The Pursuit of Attention

The Pursuit of Attention

Power and Individualism in Everyday Life

Charles Derber

OXFORD UNIVERSITY PRESS
Oxford   New York

Oxford University Press

Oxford   London   Glasgow
New York   Toronto   Melbourne   Auckland
Delhi   Bombay   Calcutta   Madras   Karachi
Kuala Lumpur   Singapore   Hong Kong   Tokyo
Nairobi   Dar es Salaam   Cape Town

and associate companies in
Beirut   Berlin   Ibadan   Mexico City   Nicosia

Library of Congress Cataloging in Publication Data
Derber, Charles.
  The pursuit of attention.
  Reprint. Originally published: Boston: G.K. Hall, © 1979
  Bibliography: p.   Includes index.
    1. Interpersonal relations. 2. Social interaction. 3. Individualism. 4. Social status.
5. Power (Social status) I. Title.
HM132.D468 1983   302   83-11442
ISBN 0-19-503368-X (pbk.)

printing, last digit: 20 19 18 17 16 15 14 13 12 11

Printed in the United States of America

To my Parents and Morrie and Ann
for attention that made this work possible

If I am not for myself, who will be for me?
But if I am for myself only, what am I?
And if not now, when?

HILLEL

. . . left remaining (is) no other nexus between
man and man than naked self-interest . . .

MARX

Contents

Acknowledgments

There have been numerous coconspirators in this project, many, no doubt, unaware of my indebtedness to them. I would be derelict if I did not acknowledge the intellectual influence of those whose critical work on individualism and class—Erich Fromm, Philip Slater, Richard Sennett, Jack Seeley, Ivan Illich, Robert Coles, and Christopher Lasch—so greatly stimulated my own thinking. Slater, Sennett, Seeley, Illich, and Coles all read and commented on the manuscript at various stages of its development, and I am grateful for their encouragement.

I owe much also to my editors, who worked so patiently on successive drafts of the manuscript. David Low's enthusiasm, devotion, and skill in helping craft a final draft deserve emphatic recognition. Yale Magrass, a talented colleague and friend, and one of those rare sociologists knowledgeable in the arts of literate writing, helped coauthor one chapter and also played an inspired role in the editing of the entire manuscript. Special thanks are due to Alfred Schenkman, president of Schenkman Publishing Company and Mary Grace Smith and Paul Wright of G. K. Hall and Company for their enthusiasm in receiving the manuscript and their personal warmth and counsel in supporting this project.

An author requires more than his share of personal attention to complete his task. I have been blessed with loving and intellectually challenging parents always supportive of my endeavors as well as many generous relatives and friends who have borne with me during periods of obsession and encouraged me in times of hesitancy and uncertainty. Those especially burdened, and to whom I owe more than these brief acknowledgments, include Brian McLaughlin, Claire Cuddy, Martha Kirschenbaum, Debbie Medansky, Gracia Woodward, Paul Weckstein, Joe Becker, Carole

Shebby, Lucy Reid, Linda Stein, Nick Sheridan, Rainy Maddallo, Nedra Shulkin, Richard Flacks, Barbara Zimbel, and especially Bruce and Edie Weitzmann-Maddi.

I owe most in this undertaking to Morrie Schwartz and Ann Cordilia. Morrie's generosity of heart and spirit, and special genius for attention giving, sustained me throughout my writing. I have drawn profligately on his faith in my ideas and his unflagging nurturance and support, for which I only hope some day to be able to reciprocate. Ann, a gifted sociologist and cherished friend, endured countless presentations of the thesis set forth here, responding not only with endless patience but with her characteristic incisiveness from which I have learned much. For her astute ideas and wisdom, and her continuing friendship, I am always grateful.

CD

Part I
Informal Dynamics

Individualism

"I was saying," continued the Rocket, "I was saying———what was I saying?"
"You were talking about yourself," replied the Roman Candle.
"Of course; I knew I was discussing some interesting subject when I was so rudely interrupted . . ."

OSCAR WILDE, from "The Remarkable Rocket"

Introduction

Without attention being exchanged and distributed, there is no social life. A unique social resource, attention is created anew in each encounter and allocated in ways deeply affecting human interactions.

The quality of any interaction depends on the tendencies of those involved to seek and share attention. Competition develops when people seek to focus attention mainly on themselves; cooperation occurs when the participants are willing and able to give it. In cooperative interactions attention is distributed to each person according to his or her needs, while in competitive interactions attention is typically dominated by those most powerful. In extreme instances, certain people monopolize attention while others do not receive even the minimum allowing them to feel included or visible.

This book explores the dynamics of attention found in American society. I have distinguished between "formal" behavior, dictated by institutionally defined status and roles, and "informal" behavior, activity not formally prescribed. In Part I, I consider the informal behavior that emerges when people have some freedom from their formal obligations, primarily in conversations with friends and acquaintances in everyday life. In studying everyday conversation, I have found a pervasive tendency for individuals to seek predominant attention for themselves. I shall suggest that this pattern is rooted in an American cultural individualism which encourages self-interest and self-absorption.

Even in informal conversations, where people do not have strictly defined roles, they are not entirely free to disregard formal status requirements.[1] Pure "informal" behavior thus does not

---

1. "Informal" interactions can be distinguished from "formal" interactions,

occur in any setting and is discussed in Part I as a model never fully realized in social life. In Part II, when I turn to "formal" behavior that occurs in both institutionally regulated interactions and in informal conversations, I explore the limits of this initial model.

In Part II, I focus on the relation between attention and status. This relation is most pronounced in the formal interactions at workplaces and other institutional settings where attention is channeled to those in authority. In all interactions, the amount of attention any individual receives is shaped by gender, social class, and other factors that determine one's worth. The dynamics of attention in America are intricately meshed with the stratification system of the society as a whole, and I shall show that inequalities in the distribution of attention are linked to broader social inequality.

The relation between the dynamics of face-to-face interaction and the larger society underlies my approach here. My focus on social interaction falls within the domain of what has traditionally been called "micro" sociology. Growing out of Georg Simmel's work on the sociology of interpersonal life and Erving Goffman's work on face-to-face relations, microsociology has been kept largely separate from "macro" sociology, which is the analysis of economic, political, social, and cultural systems. Theorists of the "micro" have typically "bracketed" or ignored the larger institutional theater where interpersonal dynamics are played. Conversely, the great traditions of "macro" sociology, including Marxism and other paradigms of historical and socioeconomic analysis, have lacked a close treatment of face-to-face interaction.

Some social theorists, however, have attempted to integrate these perspectives. C. Wright Mills and Hans Gerth, in a work receiving insufficient consideration today, developed a model for social psychology linking face-to-face dynamics and institutional systems in which "the structural and historical features of modern society [are] connected with the most intimate features of man's

---

which are those strictly organized according to institutionally defined roles and tasks, as in classrooms or psychotherapy, for example. Since people are not free of status expectations in informal conversation, "formal" behavior occurs in informal interactions. Similarly, while informal behavior occurs mainly in informal interactions, it takes place also in formal ones.

self."[2] A related framework was introduced by Erich Fromm, who argued for the development of a "dynamic" social psychology where the principal forms of interpersonal behavior, social character, and conciousness would be analyzed in relation to the dominant socioeconomic system. In a discussion that has influenced my own perspective, Fromm argued that individualism is a key factor in the organization of social relations in modern Western societies, suggesting that the norms of egoism, self-interest, and competition that prevail in the capitalist marketplace significantly affect interactions and character in the United States and other contemporary Western societies.[3]

In this book I explore dynamics of everyday face-to-face behavior within the context of the culture and socioeconomic system of American society. My focus in Part I is on the individualistic attention-behavior found especially in informal social life. By individualistic behavior, I mean self-interested, egoistic action displaying lack of concern and responsibility for others. In social interaction, one form this takes is seeking to monopolize attention. It occurs primarily in informal conversations where people are freed from institutionally defined tasks and obligations and are at liberty to focus on themselves.

In the first chapter I show that American cultural norms encourage a subtle attention to oneself, as everyone is expected to assume responsibility for his own needs and is required to take only minimal initiative to assure others' attention. Informal attention-behavior mirrors broader forms of American individualism which establish individual initiative and self-concern as primary virtues. In the second chapter I explore a set of pervasive attention-practices reflecting a psychology of self-absorption and narcissism. These all involve ways that American conversationalists act to turn the topics of ordinary conversations to themselves without showing sustained interest in others' topics. Such "conversational narcissism" is explored as the main expression of an

---

2. Hans Gerth and C. Wright Mills, *Character and Social Structure*, p. 8. [Complete details of publication for all references are given in the Bibliography.]
3. Fromm's most important works in this regard are his earlier ones: *Escape From Freedom* and *The Sane Society*.

individualistic psychology that turns much of social life in America into the pursuit of self-gratification.

Extremely individualistic societies are vulnerable to a disintegration of social life in which needs and desires for egoistic gratification overwhelm the social order. In America, the individualistic psychology underlying conversational narcissism is one of broad self-absorption, bred by cultural and economic individualism and the emergence of the "self" cut adrift from any enduring community. While I focus in Part I on the specific dynamics of conversation, I explore in the final chapter the societal conditions that encourage, indeed, require, such "self-orientation."

When we consider the formal interactions that take place in schools, workplaces and other institutions, it becomes clear that attention and status are closely linked. In the informal interactions considered in Part I, differences of status and role are less emphasized than in highly structured institutional settings. In formal interactions, the right to pursue attention for oneself and to receive it from others is conditioned by one's institutional roles and social power. I thus turn in the second part of the book to what I call the "formal" dynamics of attention, concerned with the ways that status and official power dictate attention-behavior and shape the amount of attention that people receive.

This requires going beyond the work of Goffman and others who have explored status and deference in interpersonal life toward an analysis of the ways that face-to-face relations are uniquely embedded within the dominant socioeconomic system— in this instance, within the patriarchal system and class structure of contemporary America. I have indicated that microsociologists have neglected analysis of the larger economic and political institutions. Face-to-face behavior always takes place, however, within a larger societal context. I show in Part II that the allocation and distribution of attention, much like the allocation and distribution of wealth, is uniquely structured by the prevailing socioeconomic system, reflecting pervasive hierarchical patterns of power and prestige.

While I remain focused on the ways that people give and get attention, the analysis in Part II moves back and forth between the structure of face-to-face relations and features of larger institutions. I show that patriarchy and the class system lead to important differences between men and women and between dominant and subordinate economic groupings in ways of exchanging attention and prospects of receiving it. Women and members of subordinate socioeconomic groups are assigned roles that require the subordination of self and the giving of attention. Their psychology and attention-behavior thus vary from the patterns discussed in Part I and are analyzed as key face-to-face expressions of social inequality.

The analysis in this book is based on research carried out by the author examining the exchange and distribution of attention in social interactions. The original study, the "Attention-Interaction Project," involved field studies of face-to-face interactions in six designated settings: family households, workplaces, restaurants, classrooms, dormitories, and therapy groups. Trained observers, working from a standardized observation guide, studied fifteen hundred interactions in these settings, focusing on the amount of visual and topical[4] attention given each participant and factors determining who receives the most and least attention.

The observers wrote qualitative accounts of the following: (1) the differing personality and interactional styles of those at the top and bottom of the "attention-hierarchy," (2) the effect of gender and social status on the ability of each participant to gain and hold attention, (3) the kinds of competition for attention and the ways in which they were resolved, (4) the relation between the institutional roles and power of each participant and the attention he or she received, (5) the relative equality or inequality in the distribution of attention, (6) factors creating extreme inequality, and (7) the relative disposition of each participant to seek attention for himself or herself. Carried out in natural settings, these observations provide rich source material about attention in a wide variety of ordinary interactions. I have drawn extensively on them as preliminary evidence and illustrative data for the hypotheses and ideas advanced throughout the book.[5]

---

4. See p. 11.
5. To insure the "naturalness" of the interactions, those observed were not told of the study nor informed that they were being observed. Strict confidentiality of the observational reports was maintained and the identity of those observed, when known to the observer, was not recorded on the

The second project involved the tape-recording and transcription of one hundred informal dinner conversations among acquaintances and friends in restaurants, dining halls, and households. Each conversation involved the participation of different volunteers; altogether, the study involved the participation of 320 conversationalists.[6]

These transcripts permitted a more precise analysis of the exchange and distribution of attention in conversation. Special consideration was given to whose topics were discussed and the specific processes by which people seek to turn the conversation to themselves. These transcripts provided extensive and detailed raw conversational data for interpreting individualistic attention-behavior.

This study is an exploratory effort to develop methods of social analysis and derive conclusions concerning the relation of face-to-face processes to larger institutions. The analysis of attention offers a methodology for exploring the psychology and social relations bred by individualism and the nature of power and status in everyday life. Such an investigation can hopefully point to a comprehensive social theory illuminating everyday life in America as an expression of its dominant cultural traditions and political economy.

---

report. Observation focused on the attention-dynamics and only indirectly on the content of what was being said. The reports do not include detailed accounts of the substance of the conversation; they do include notes on how long, and by what process, each person held the focus of attention, but are only schematic in regard to the specific development of topics.

6. Volunteers were drawn from students, faculty, and nonprofessional white-collar and blue-collar employees from three university communities in the Boston area. The volunteers were informed that the study was concerned with aspects of ordinary social interaction, but were not told specifically of the focus on attention. After their conversation was completed, they were fully informed of the nature and purpose of the study.

Chapter 1

Every Man for Himself; Every Woman for Herself: *Individualism Face-to-Face*

Each individual is conscious of himself, *but nobody is conscious of themselves collectively. . . .*

THOMAS HARDY, from *The Woodlanders*

Psychologists have treated attention as a fundamental human need. John Bowlby and René Spitz, for example, while studying the emotional development of infants, concluded that the baby's need for attention is similar to that for food.[1] Infants who receive less than a required minimum of attention may die or develop grotesque physical and emotional aberrations.

R. D. Laing, in early studies of adult psychiatric patients, found a common preoccupation with being seen or simply being noticed.[2] He showed that emotional deterioration frequently results from a form of attention-starvation and that psychotic symptoms can in many cases be pinpointed as obsessive attention fantasies. The paranoid person who feels that everyone is looking at or talking about him may simply be creating in his imagination the attention lacking in his everyday life. The "Napoleonic Complex" and other delusions of grandeur are extreme ways to overcome the feeling of never being noticed.

What distinguishes Laing's patients is not the need for attention but a disadvantage in claiming the amount or kind that permits others to maintain sanity. Most people have desires or needs for attention which they seek to satisfy in everyday life. People differ mainly in their success in gratifying their needs.

In this book I am not concerned with attention as a psychological need per se, but rather with the social conditions that affect how much attention people seek to gain and determine how much different people receive.[3] The rules governing the exchange of attention are a basic feature of each society's culture and as such reveal much about its fundamental assumptions. Who gets attention—in individual face-to-face encounters and in institutional arenas like the family or the workplace—is closely linked to social power and illuminates the status hierarchy of society.

---

1. John Bowlby, *Maternal Care and Mental Health*. René Spitz, "Anaclitic Depression," in *Psychoanalytic Study of the Child*.
2. R. D. Laing, *The Divided Self*.
3. No position is taken here regarding a theory of psychological needs or the status of attention as an elementary psychological requirement. Psychological theories are vague regarding the social and biological origins of needs and are not easily reconciled with the finding that what constitutes "satisfaction" of a need appears to vary significantly in different cultures. Whether a need for attention exists among adults in all cultures is not a central concern here. The focus is rather on the social factors governing how attention is exchanged and distributed in everyday life.

Attention and the Structure of Face-to-Face Interaction

Attention is given and received in all interactions, whether it be lovemaking, informal conversation, or encounters at work. While people can be the object of attention outside the context of face-to-face interaction—on television, over the phone, or as the object of another's thinking—I am concerned here only with face-to-face attention. I shall concentrate especially on a form to be called "focused" or "commonly focused" attention.

Commonly focused attention is the kind exchanged in "focused" interaction, defined by Erving Goffman as ". . . the kind of interaction that occurs when people gather close together and openly cooperate to sustain a single focus of attention, typically by taking turns at talking."[4] Focused interactions are mainly conversations—both informal and those regulated by institutinally defined roles. These can be distinguished from "unfocused" interactions where people simply pass in and out of each other's view.[5] The unique feature of focused interaction is the development of a common focus of attention. There are both a visual and cognitive common focus of attention in conversation. The visual focus is the person being looked at, normally the person speaking. The cognitive focus is the person being talked about, the person or object who is the topic or "subject" of the conversation.[6]

4. Erving Goffman, *Behavior in Public Places*, p. 24.
5. Unfocused interactions take place in public settings such as subway cars and waiting rooms where strangers are physically together but are not conversing. Goffman (*Behavior in Public Places*, Chapter 2) also identifies a third kind of interaction which he calls "partly focused." This involves situations in which certain participants are talking while others are present but formally excluded from the right to take part. An example is the interaction in a restaurant in which the waiter is expected to keep an eye on his customers but not to take part in their conversation. Aspects of the allocation of attention in "unfocused" and "partly focused" interactions are given some consideration in the second part of this book. Throughout, however, the main concern is with the dynamics of focused interaction.
6. The definitions of the visual and cognitive focus require further explication. In all verbal interaction, the common visual focus at any given moment is occupied by the person talking. Over the course of an entire interaction, the person who speaks the most receives the most "visual" attention. However, the identification of talking with visual attention has certain limitations, particularly in two-person interactions, as each person looks at the other and not at a common object. Thus it is not possible to speak of a visual focus. To say that the person talking is the person receiving

The question of who should be the focus—and how much visual and cognitive attention each person should receive—arises in every social interaction. Thus, as with economic resources, there is a problem of allocating and distributing attention. Accordingly, one can ask the following kinds of questions: How much equality exists in the amount of attention given to different participants? Are there interactional classes of "rich" and "poor" corresponding to those who typically receive large and small shares of attention? Is attention allocated on a cooperative or competitive basis? Every society evolves a set of rules for organizing and allocating attention which reflects a particular way of answering these questions.

Different attention dynamics develop in informal and formal interactions. Informal interactions are those in which people do not have institutionally defined roles or tasks to perform. These include all the ordinary conversations that take place among friends and acquaintances in everyday life. Formal interactions are ones tightly structured by institutionally defined roles and tasks, such as interactions in the classroom or doctor's office. In these interactions, who gets attention is determined differently than in informal interactions, largely by the organization and requirements of the roles themselves.[7]

---

visual focus is an extension from three or more person interaction, where a common visual focus does exist and is normally centered on the person speaking.

The term cognitive attention derives from the condition of being at the center of others' cognition or thought. In conversation, a person receives "cognitive" focus whenever the topic is focused on himself or herself. Most ordinary conversation is about one or another of the conversationalists. The allocation of cognitive attention thus concerns who will become the predominant subject or topic of the conversation. If the focus is on some abstract topic or on a person not present, then none of the conversationalists involved receives cognitive focus.

While my concern is primarily with verbal interaction, it should be pointed out that cognitive and visual attention can also be exchanged in nonverbal interaction. When lovers look into each others' eyes without speaking, they are exchanging visual attention. The cognitive focus in nonverbal interaction is the person who is the subject or center of both persons' awareness (that is, the person being thought about by both persons). Thus, in mother-infant interaction, the child receives predominant cognitive focus as the awareness of both is centered on him. In conversation, the cognitive focus is the person being talked about; in nonverbal interaction, it is the one being thought about or the common object of mental awareness.

7. The discussion of allocation in formal interaction is reserved for Part II, beginning on pp. 40 ff.

Informal Interaction and Individual Initiative

The informal attention-behavior that occurs in everyday conversations in America is individualistic and mirrors broader forms of individualism in American life. In an individualistic culture, each person must assume responsibility primarily for himself or herself.[8] In America, the dominant culture of individualism has traditionally emphasized competition and individual initiative as principles of social conduct.[9] Allocation of attention is associated with special forms of individual responsibility and competition.

Who gets attention in informal conversation is determined primarily by competing individual initiatives. Each individual is responsible for himself, with his share of attention determined largely by his own efforts and skills. Each is relatively free, within the limits of civility, to take as much initiative as desired and to command as much of the attention as he can.[10]

8. The concept of individualism has been used not only to characterize cultural systems, but economic systems, philosophical and political traditions, and psychological dispositions. It is thus associated with a wide range of meanings in different contexts. These include the idea of "egoism" in philosophical and psychological thinking, the freedom of the individual in political individualism, and laissez faire and individual initiative in economic behavior. Of special interest here are forms of cultural and social individualism that define patterns of responsibility and concern for self and others. The emphasis on principles of individual responsibility and self-interest underlie most forms of individualism. Because of the nature of the subject matter, I am also centrally concerned with social psychological expressions of individualism that reflect "self-orientation" or a primary concern with the self (egoism). This is elaborated in the second chapter. For a brief review of the different meanings of individualism, see Steven Lukes, *Individualism*.
9. The dominant culture of individualism in American society has its roots in economic, religious, and social conditions. Most observers have stressed the relation of American individualism to American capitalism and the ways in which economic individualism breeds individualistic social ideology and cultural patterns. Others have stressed the importance of the Protestant cultural heritage as well as the special patterns of mobility, transcience, and isolation from established community that characterized frontier life. Following Erich Fromm, I have regarded economic individualism as of special importance and have developed certain parallels between economic and social and psychological modes of individualism. See Erich Fromm, *Escape From Freedom*.
10. I discuss the ritual restraints of the civil order in Chapter 2 on pp. 23 ff. The "freedom" in informal interaction contrasts with the regimentation in formal interaction. In formal settings, such as the classroom, people are expected to take a prescribed amount of initiative consistent with their

The term "initiative" is used here to mean any active assertion to gain or keep attention. Efforts to attract attention can be called *gaining initiatives* and include moves to gain the floor or to introduce one's own topics. Efforts to hold the attention once it is gotten, either by continuing to speak or prolonging one's topics can be called *sustaining initiatives.* How much attention anyone receives is decided primarily by the frequency and persistence of both types of initiatives and their success in competition with others.[11]

People vary in aggressiveness and style because of differences in personality, gender, and social status. Certain individuals seek the floor more boldly than others and introduce their own topics more forcefully. Some people are more animated, dramatic, or expressive, traits which contribute to success in both winning the floor and holding it. Furthermore, as the content of what is said clearly affects how others respond, intelligence, humor, and sensitivity all bear on the effectiveness of gaining and sustaining initiatives.

Individualism and Competition

In America, informal attention-behavior is individualistic in the sense that each person takes initiative for his or her share without assuming responsibility for others. As long as they observe the norms of civility, people are free to concentrate on the gratifi-

institutional role. While there is much greater discretion in informal interaction, the freedom is not absolute. Differences in status create different
expectations of behavior, with those of higher status normally freer to take
more initiatives on their own behalf. The "free initiative" in informal
interaction is thus only relative; the limitations associated with status
differences are discussed in Part II, where I discuss these "formal" aspects of
behavior in informal interactions.
11. Success here means actual effectiveness in gaining or holding attention
when one seeks to do so. It should be noted that an individual can receive
attention without taking any initiative, as when another conversationalist
introduces topics about him or persists in directing attention to him by asking
repeated questions. The fundamental characteristic of the individual initiative
system is not that it excludes such attention-giving behavior from others but
(a) that it places people under minimal and purely ritualized obligations to
initiate this behavior and (b) that it gives no one the right to expect any
attention other than that which comes through his or her own initiative.

cation of their own needs.[12] We can understand this more precisely by distinguishing between *attention-getting* initiatives (the gaining- and sustaining-initiatives already discussed) and *attention-giving* initiatives. Attention-giving initiatives are designed to steer attention to others and include active efforts to introduce topics about them or to support their subjects already set forth. Except under special circumstances, as when someone expresses pain or great distress, conversationalists are not required to make any attention-giving initiatives. This is reflected in the tendency to initiate topics about oneself far more often than about others, as shown clearly in the dinner conversation interpreted below.

Topic Number	Topic Subject	Topic-Initiator
1.	Dan's plans for the evening	Dan
2.	Food	Jim
3.	Dinner schedule	Kay
4.	Kay's art work	Jim
5.	Food	Dan
6.	Kay's job	Kay
7.	Jim's job	Jim
8.	Dan's lunch	Dan
9.	Dan's afternoon conversation	Dan
10.	Food	Kay

With one exception, each topic about one of the participants is initiated by that person himself or herself. In my analysis of one hundred dinner conversations this pattern is the characteristic one.[13] People concentrate on initiating topics about themselves and assume that others will do the same.[14]

This does not mean, however, that conversationalists are not under any obligation to give attention. People are expected to indicate that they are listening while others are speaking, either by

12. The essential individualism of the system is effectively masked by the civil norms that demand that people maintain an appearance of interest in and concern for others. Tensions exist between the rituals of sociability and the underlying individualistic imperatives of the attention-system. The ritual system is explored at some length in the next chapter.

13. In ninety percent of the conversations, at least two-thirds of the topics focusing on one of the participants are initiated by that person. From the study of dinner conversations described on p 8.

14. These observations are drawn from the study of dinner conversations described on p. 8.

looking at them and nodding or by making acknowledgments such as "mmm" or "uh huh."[15] In addition, there are even certain obligations of polite initiative-taking to assure others of minimal attention. One is the mandatory ritual at the onset of conversations to express interest in others through inquiries such as "How are you?" Such expressions maintain civility and assure each conversationalist a ritual quotient of attention that I call "civil attention." This includes initial eye contact that indicates inclusion as a participant as well as greetings. It entails over the full course of a conversation the right to complete a sentence or brief thought, to get eye contact from others while speaking, and to expect that other speakers will not blatantly ignore one's interests, ideas, or reactions.

Everyone is in a competitive position in a conversation because the amount of attention received depends on the relative success of one's own initiatives to attract and hold the common focus.[16] Commonly focused attention within any interaction is limited and can become "scarce" if the amount any person seeks is greater than that available.[17] Under conditions of unusual scarcity, the

---

15. Obligations regarding responsiveness entail not only a demonstration that one is listening, but a minimal measure of supportive behavior that indicates some interest or at least a willingness to acknowledge the topic of the other. One must distinguish between these required civil responses, which give the speaker the freedom to continue his or her initiatives without blatant interruptions and discretionary efforts by the listener to support the topic of the speaker beyond ritual acknowledgments that he or she is paying attention. Subtle differences in responsiveness significantly affect the extent to which a topic is kept alive. The civil obligations regarding responsiveness indicate that the responsibility for sustaining topics on the floor is not entirely individualized, although it lies predominantly with the initiator.

16. This does not imply that all people constantly compete for attention. While people do frequently compete, many do not either because they do not desire attention in a particular interaction or because they prefer to take initiative only when it is clear that others are not seeking attention themselves. The attitude of the individual must be distinguished from the structure of the allocation system. An analogy can be made with a competitive sport or game in which the players are in a competitive position with one another, but the individual players may be either highly competitive or relatively competitive, or not at all competitive.

17. While attention is not intrinsically "scarce," it tends to become so under the individualistic conditions of allocation and distribution described here. The individualistic attention-norms sanction self-oriented behavior and legitimate efforts to focus attention on oneself. When this becomes the prevailing pattern—and characterizes many of the participants in normal interactions—

competitive features become more visible and pronounced. The participants—in large groups, for example—may openly vie with one another to gain the floor by interrupting or shouting one another down. However, in most settings the competition remains disguised because they are expected to be more subtle and discreet.

The Problem of Invisibility

There is a striking parallel between the individualistic and competitive processes of attention-getting and certain forms of economic behavior. In a classic capitalist economic model rewards are allocated through competitive individual initiative with no limits placed on what share of the total rewards (within a given market) any individual (or firm) can gain. This leads to inequalities determined by relative competitive power rather than needs. Similarly, in informal interactions there is no assurance that each individual will get the attention he wants because competitive individual initiative again decides allocation, with no limits on how much (or how little) anyone should receive. Certain people can dominate or monopolize the attention while others may be unsuccessful in claiming even the minimal share required to feel included.

Poverty has an interactional parallel in "invisibility," where one or more listeners can gain hardly any attention. It occurs when the norms of face-to-face behavior offer insufficient protection against being ignored or overlooked. The "invisible" person does not gain even the minimum attention required to feel that his or her presence has been acknowledged and established.

In America the norms governing informal conversation do not require anyone to give attention to persons who, for reasons of personality or social status, are unable to command it through their own initiatives. While each conversationalist is assured a minimal amount of civil attention, some people experience difficulty in making themselves visible in ordinary talk. For example:

---

attention becomes scarce in ordinary conversation, as each person seeks a predominant share of the attention for himself. This theme is analyzed in depth in the next chapter.

Five people are sitting eating lunch. They are engaged
in a lively conversation about changes in marriage.
Four of the five take an active role, breaking in frequently with comments about themselves and their experiences in relationships. The fifth member, Bill, who
is less forceful and self-assured than the others, has
trouble gaining the floor. He makes several efforts to
speak, but someone louder or more persistent inter-
rupts each time and he gives way. The third or fourth
time this happens, he becomes very agitated and abruptly turns to the woman next to him to initiate a side
conversation. He begins to tell her what he wanted to
say to the group. She gives him eye contact and listens
for about a minute, but then her attention is captured
by what someone in the main discussion is saying and
so, touching his arm briefly, turns back to the others.
He also turns his attention back to the main conversation, but makes no further efforts to speak and does
not get any attention from the others. [18]

A variety of personality traits can render an individual vulnerable to this kind of invisibility. Being less assertive, aggressive, or
animated, or especially shy or insecure often leads to difficulties in
getting attention.[19] In the illustration above, lack of forcefulness
and self-assurance became a major handicap in what was a spirited
competition for the floor. Bill was extended no help or support
through openings from the others and was forced to rely on his
own initiatives. The attempt to initiate a side conversation, his
way of seeking to win at least some marginal attention, succeeded
only briefly in relieving his invisibility in the main conversation.

Observations of informal conversations in restaurants and living

18. From the Attention-Interaction Project supervised by the author. See
p. 7.
19. Conversely, other personality characteristics are extremely important in
gaining attention. The qualities cited most often by observers in the
attention-interaction study as characteristic of those winning attention
include assertiveness, aggressiveness, animatedness, self-confidence, authoritativeness, and humor. While these qualities are effective in the gaining of
attention under conditions of individualism, they are not necessarily more
compelling in all cultures. The specific norms of attention-behavior, as well as
the particular personality qualities prized in each culture, may lead to
different kinds of personalities winning attention in different societies.

rooms suggest that an unequal distribution of attention typically develops. As the number of people increases, it is more likely that one or more will get little or no attention, this being reported frequently in conversations involving more than two people.[20] Invisibility is thus a common experience, although usually unseen by those free of it, as there are no routine means by which invisible participants can call attention to their state.[21]

In conversations between two people attention is less scarce and problems of invisibility less intractable. Nonetheless, one of the conversationalists can fade into invisibility if the other monopolizes the talking time or keeps the topic always focused on himself or herself. There are ritual prohibitions against such behavior reflected in apologies when blatantly violated. Common ones are "Oh, I see I've done nothing but talk about myself," or "Gee, I hope I haven't bored you with all these personal problems." If there is still time, the offender may extend an opening to the other; "Well, enough about myself. What have you been up to?" or "Now I want to hear all about you." However, because these offerings frequently are made near the end of conversation, they may serve to make ritual amends without significantly increasing reciprocity. Moreover, the offender often remains completely unaware of the other's invisibility and even the victim, as long as his or her rights to civil attention have been fulfilled, may only come to realize afterward that the conversation has never stayed on his or her topics.

---

20. From the Attention-Interaction Project. Not only was invisibility a common occurrence, but domination of attention by one of the particpants was observed in a majority of the conversations. In three-fourths of the conversations a significant inequality in the distribution of attention was reported, with one person described as clearly dominant in over fifty percent of the conversations.

21. In special interactional settings, such as therapy groups, the dynamics of the interaction are themselves a legitimate subject of conversation and it becomes easier for those getting no attention to raise this as a problem for the consideration of the others involved. It is not unusual for members of therapy or counseling groups to complain of not being sufficiently appreciated or noticed. Philip Slater, in personal communication, suggested that the issue of their own invisibility is the most common way that invisible persons in such settings may be able to get any attention. In ordinary conversation, however, awareness of the interactional dynamics of the conversation itself normally remains covert and is introduced explicitly into the conversation only if the ritual order has been blatantly violated or the relationship of those involved has been specifically defined to encompass open consideration of these matters.

Chapter 2

Monopolizing the Conversation:
On Being Civilly Egocentric

"Conversation indeed" said the Rocket. "You have talked the whole time yourself. That is not conversation."
"Somebody must listen" answered the Frog, "and I like to do all the talking myself."
"You are a very irritating person" said the Rocket, "and very ill bred. I hate people who talk about themselves, as you do, when one wants to talk about oneself, as I do . . ."

OSCAR WILDE, from "The Remarkable Rocket"

Individualism has a counterpart in American psychology. People tend to seek attention for themselves in face-to-face interactions. This attention-getting psychology reflects an underlying character structure of "self-orientation" that emerges in highly individualistic societies.[1] Erich Fromm has theorized that a shared character structure develops in each society, a "social character" that is a response to the requirements of the social order and best suited for survival and success within it. The self-oriented character type develops a highly egocentric view of the world and is motivated primarily by self-interest. To cope with social and economic insecurity bred by individualism, he becomes preoccupied with himself. His "attention-getting" psychology is thus

---

1. In contrast, an "attention-giving" psychology is based on the tendency for the individual to focus attention on the needs and concerns of others as well as himself in social life. While the attention-getting psychology is more consistent with the individualistic norms of the dominant culture and is more pervasive in the society, the attention-giving psychology is expected of members of subordinate groups, especially women, and tends to characterize their behavior in face-to-face interactions with those more powerful.

While a dominant psychology of attention develops in every culture, there is thus significant variation by sex and social status. I am concerned in this rooted in a broad self-absorption engendered by social conditions highly developed in contemporary America.[2]

In informal conversation, the self-oriented person repeatedly seeks to turn attention to himself. This "conversational narcissism" is closely related to the individualistic norms already discussed. As shown in the first chapter, attention is allocated according to norms in which each individual is responsible for himself, and is free, within limits of civility, to take as much as he can. These norms legitimate focusing on one's own needs in informal talk and are consistent with the effort by self-oriented conversationalists to gain predominant attention for themselves.

The Forms of Conversational Narcissism

Conversational narcissism is the key manifestation of the dominant attention-getting psychology in America. It occurs in in-

---

chapter only with the dominant form in American culture. In the second part of the book I examine the variations among groups who occupy different positions in the social structure.

2. In his classic work, *Escape From Freedom,* Fromm discussed the concept of social character and emphasized the primacy of individualism in shaping character structure in modern capitalist cultures. The theme of egoism has been central in many analyses of the psychology bred by individualism. In his work on suicide, Durkheim treated egoism as a response to the weakening of social bonds and traditional collectivities. The disaffiliated individual is centrally self-oriented as his isolation breeds self-absorption and his individualized social and economic position erodes collective purposes and engenders preoccupation with his own needs.

Several American social theorists have recently pointed to the emergence of self-orientation as a central element in American social character. Philip Reiff has discussed "psychological man"—a character type bred by modern individualism and concerned primarily with his own personal growth and gratification. Richard Sennett has discussed the fall of "public man" and the rise of the more self-oriented and private man of contemporary culture. Christopher Lasch has spoken of the growth of the narcissistic character as a response to the survival pressures of contemporary individualism. The breakdown of family life and other community supports and the burdening of each individual with economic and social responsibilities formerly shared with others necessarily generates a focus on oneself and preoccupation with one's own needs. These themes are elaborated in the last chapter. See Émile Durkheim, *Suicide,* Philip Reiff, *The Triumph of the Therapeutic,* Richard Sennett, *The Fall of Public Man,* Christopher Lasch, *The Culture of Narcissism.*

formal conversations among friends, family and coworkers. The profusion of popular literature about listening and the etiquette of managing those who talk constantly about themselves suggests its pervasiveness in everyday life; its contemporary importance is indicated by the early appearance of these problems in the most recent edition of Emily Post's etiquette manual.[3]

In observations of ordinary conversations, I have found a set of extremely common conversational practices which show an unresponsiveness to others' topics and involve turning them into one's own.[4] Because of norms prohibiting blatantly egocentric behavior, these practices are often exquisitely subtle; ritual forms of civility and face-saving have evolved to limit the overt expression of egoism in social life.[5] Although conversationalists are free to introduce topics about themselves, they are expected to maintain an appearance of genuine interest in those about others in the conversation. A delicate face-saving system requires that people refrain from openly disregarding others' concerns and keep expressions of disinterest from becoming visible. Practices of conversational narcissism are normally, then, driven underground and expressed in disguised forms where they are not readily discerned by any member of the conversation.[6]

To explore the narcissistic practices that occur most often, we must distinguish between two kinds of attention-response: the *shift-response* and the *support-response*. The shift- and support-responses are alternative ways one can react to others' conversational initiatives. The differences between the two can be seen in the following examples:[7]

---

3. See Emily Post, *Etiquette*, Chapter 1.
4. These studies are described in the Introduction, pp. 7-8.
5. The ritual order has been richly described by Erving Goffman, "Face-Work," in *Interaction Ritual*.
6. This unawareness may extend to the self-oriented individual himself. Conversational narcissism is typically not conscious behavior but reflects rather a habitual focus on or absorption with oneself that is non-self-consciously expressed in conversational patterns. Use of terminology such as conversational initiatives or strategies should thus not be understood as always referring to willful or manipulative behavior but to unreflective behavior that has the effect of creating shifts in topic and attention.
7. The illustrations of shift-responses here are drawn from the transcriptions of the dinner conversations (see p. 8). The support-responses here are hypothetical, presented in this format to highlight the contrast with shift-

John: I'm feeling really starved.
Mary: Oh, I just ate. (shift-response)
John: I'm feeling really starved.
Mary: When was the last time you ate? (support-response)

John: God, I'm feeling so angry at Bob.
Mary: Yeah, I've been feeling the same way toward him. (shift-response)
John: God, I'm feeling so angry at Bob.
Mary: Why, what's been going on between the two of you? (support-response)

John: My mother would pack me melted cheese sandwiches every day.
Mary: My mom never made me a lunch I could stand to eat. (shift-response)
John: My mother would pack me melted cheese sandwiches every day.
Mary: Hey, your mother was all right. (support-response)

John: I saw Jane today on the street.
Mary: I haven't seen her in a week. (shift-response)
John: I saw Jane today on the street.
Mary: Oh, how's she doing? (support-response)

John: I just love Brahms.
Mary: Chopin's my favorite. (shift-response)
John: I just love Brahms.
Mary: Which is your favorite piece? (support-response)

The shift-response and support-response are both commonly used. They are superficially so little different that few conversationalists notice the distinction. Yet they affect the flow of attention and the development of topics in markedly different ways. When Mary uses the shift-response, she temporarily shifts the attention to herself and creates the potential for a change in

---

responses. Unless otherwise indicated, all examples presented in the text in this chapter are drawn from the transcripts. For purposes of readability, the presentation of the transcripts is nontechnical and does not include special markings denoting pauses or interruptions.

topic. When using the support-response, she keeps the attention and topic securely focused on John.

Of the two responses, only the shift-response changes who is the subject of the conversation. For example, if Mary says to John, "I'm going to the movies tonight," John can temporarily make himself the subject with any of the following replies:

That reminds me, I've got to go home tonight.
I'm sick of movies these days.
Gee, I wonder what I'm going to do tonight.

With each of these shift-responses, John introduces the dilemma of whether the conversation will continue with Mary as the subject or will turn to him. Alternatively, he could offer the following kinds of support responses:

What movie?
Great, you deserve a break.
Are you feeling good enough to go?

These support-responses are attention-giving ones not in competition with Mary's initial assertion. They keep the conversation clearly focused on her and give her license to continue as the subject. Support-responses, unlike shift-responses, cannot normally be introduced to transfer attention to the self.[8]

Conversational narcissism involves preferential use of the shift-response and underutilization of the support-response. We can distinguish between active and passive narcissistic practices. The active practices involve repeated use of the shift-response to subtly turn the topics of others into topics about oneself. The passive practices involve minimal use of support-responses so that others' topics are not sufficiently reinforced and so are terminated prematurely.

---

8. Under special circumstances, a support-response can be used as an attention-getting initiative by subtly redirecting the conversation. By asking a certain form of question about the other, for example, the respondent may steer the talk toward new ideas, leading eventually toward a focus on himself. However, it cannot lead to a shift in the next turn in the conversation, and normally sustains the talk on the other's topic for at least several successive turns.

ACTIVE PRACTICES

The shift-response is the one response to another's initiative through which one can introduce one's own topic. While it does not necessarily change the topic—and is frequently not so intended—it nonetheless always creates the possibility. The following dialogue illustrates how the shift-response is typically used by self-oriented conversationalists to bring attention to themselves:

> *Mary:* My summer place has been such a blessing this year.
> *John:* I know, I sure would like a place like that, the way I've been feeling, but I've got to earn the bread first, you know?
> *Mary:* Yeah.
> *John:* I figure that if I work enough this year and next, I'll be able to check that place out in Vermont again and maybe . . .

Although John appears, in his first response, to have expanded on Mary's topic, he has subtly shifted the attention to himself. He has not responded directly to her feelings, but has shifted the conversation to his own state of mind, his problems with money, and his desires for a summer place of his own. Rather than returning to her topic, Mary then responds with a support-response allowing John in the following turn to consolidate his earlier topical initiative.

While changing the topic, John links his response to Mary's and prefaces his own with an acknowledgment of hers. The preface is a token gesture of recognition of what the other has said. Numerous other prefaces such as "oh really," "huh," "isn't that something," "same here," and "I can't believe it" recur in conversations. They soften the transition in topic and help to protect the individual against charges of unresponsiveness. A preface acknowledges that one is paying attention to the previous statement and adds legitimacy to an assertion in which the individual suddenly introduces himself as the subject. It also presents the interjection of oneself as not simply an effort to gain attention, but rather a

form of responsiveness to share personal experience or information.[9]

Although important for maintaining civility, a shift-response
does not require a preface. For example:

> *John:* I've got such a huge appetite.
> *Bill:* I couldn't eat a thing.

> *John:* My father would take me every two weeks to a
> game and I spent every minute looking forward to it.
> *Bill:* I remember the first game my father took me to.
> I made so much noise that he didn't want to take me
> anymore.

Here, the shifts in focus are legitimized by the appearance of a
topical connection. The subtlety of the shift-response is that it is
always based on a connection to the previous subject. This creates
an opening for the respondent to shift the topic to himself while
still preserving the "face" of the other.

While repeating the shift-response in the most common way
self-oriented conversationalists seek attention, it does not always
imply conversational narcissism. The shift-response can serve
either as a sharing-response or as a narcissistic topical initiative.
The major difference lies not in introducing the shift-response, but
in the intent and the statements which follow. When serving
narcissistic ends, shift-responses are repeated until a clear shift in
subject has transpired. When meant only as sharing-responses,
interjecting oneself is temporary and is quickly followed by
returning to the original topic. In these instances, the shift-
response only briefly brings attention to oneself as a means of
furthering the conversation.

---

9. That the shift-response is, in fact, often intended as a sharing-response and
not as a vehicle to shift topics renders this more plausible. The distinction
between the shift-response as a sharing response and as an attention-getting
initiative is considered in the following pages. It can be pointed out here that
when used for narcissistic purposes of topical initiative, it has attributes of
what Reusch has called a tangential response, a speech act which gives the
impression of being responsive but does not actually affirm or validate what
the other has just said. See Reusch, "The Tangential Response," in Hoch and
Zubin (eds.), *Psychopathology of Communication.*

The effectiveness of the shift-response as an attention-getting device lies partly in the difficulty in distinguishing immediately whether a given response is a sharing one or a narcissistic initiative. At a certain stage in the development of another's topic, it becomes appropriate to introduce information about oneself, but normally not until the other has introduced most of his information or narrative. The earlier the initial shift-response, the more likely it foreshadows an effort to seize the conversation.[10] This is illustrated in the following conversation:

> *Mary:* I saw the most beautiful rainbow today.
> *John:* Wow, I saw a lovely one just last week.

At this point, Mary cannot know whether John actually is interested in her experience or in simply turning the talk to himself. His statement is connected to hers and may well represent an honest attempt to share his experience or to highlight hers. But it may also signal a narcissistic initiative, which would be confirmed if he persists in using the shift response.

> *Mary:* I saw the most beautiful rainbow today.
> *John:* Wow, I saw a lovely one just last week.
> *Mary:* It had such a magnificent blend of blues and golds.
> *John:* Huh, the one I saw was all reds and yellows.

John's repeated shift responses have now become a competing initiative that make it more difficult for Mary to sustain her own subject. A decisive topical shift occurs in the next turn as Mary, despite her option to continue with her own topic, accommodates John's initiative with a support-response:

> *Mary:* I saw the most beautiful rainbow today.
> *John:* Wow, I saw such a lovely one last week.

---

10. There may be certain topics where it is legitimate to introduce oneself into the conversation immediately (for example, to provide certain necessary information for the further unfolding of the topic). The openness in the unfolding of topics and the looseness in the rules regarding the phase at which it is legitimate to introduce the self as subject in talk about others' topics creates the possibility for the exploitation of the shift-response for narcissistic ends.

> *Mary:* It had such a magnificent blend of blues and golds.
> *John:* Huh, the one I saw was all reds and yellows.
> *Mary:* What time of day did you see it?
> *John:* Early afternoon. I was walking near the river and . . .

The active narcissistic practice always follows some variation of this pattern, in which repetitions of the shift-response turns the conversation to oneself. The shift-response functions as a gaining-initiative[11] which introduces one's own topic. It sets the stage for a topic competition which will persist as long as each conversationalist continues to use a shift-response. The self-oriented conversationalist triumphs in this competition when his shift-response succeeds in eliciting a succession of support-responses from others, thus securing their acquiescence to his topic.

Incessant use of the shift-response is not typical because it is too baldy egoistic and disruptive. A more acceptable—and more pervasive—approach is one where a conversationalist makes temporary responsive concessions to others' topics before intervening to turn the focus back to himself. The self-oriented conversationalist mixes shift-responses with support-responses, leaving the impression that he has interest in others as well as himself

> *Jim:* You know, I've been wanting to get a car for so long.
> *Bill:* Yeah. (support-response)
> *Jim:* Maybe when I get the job this summer, I'll finally buy one. But they're so expensive.
> *Bill:* I was just thinking about how much I spend on my car. I think over $1500 a year. You know I had to lay out over $750 for insurance. And $250 for that fender job. (shift-response)
> *Jim:* Yeah, it's absurd. (support-response)
> *Bill:* I'm sick of cars. I've been thinking of getting a bicycle and getting around in a healthy way. I saw a great red racer up in that bike shop on Parkhurst Ave.
> *Jim:* I love bikes. But I'm just really feeling a need for

---

11. see p. 15.

a car now. I want to be able to drive up the coast
whenever I want. (shift-response)
Bill: Uh huh . . . (support-response)
Jim: I could really get into a convertible.
Bill: Oh, you can go anywhere on a bike. I'm going to
borrow John's bike and go way up north next week-
end. You know, a couple of weekends ago Sue and I
rented bikes and rode down toward the Cape . . .
(shift-response)

The narcissistic initiative and the ensuing topic competition is
subtle here. From a casual reading of the transcript there appears
to be a responsive exchange with no readily discernible egocentricity. But a more careful examination reveals the familiar
narcissistic pattern. Bill responds initially to Jim's topic with a
support-response that indicates acknowledgment and at least
minimal interest. Most of his subsequent responses, however, are
shift-responses that change the topic from Jim's desires for a new
car to a discussion of his own car and then to his own interest in
bicycles. Jim makes several efforts to steer the conversation back
to his original concern, but Bill's attention-getting initiatives are
successful. In the end, he launches into a story about his bike trip,
which decisively shifts the topic to himself.

This interchange exemplifies the pattern of active conversational narcissism. One conversationalist transforms another's
topic into one pertaining to himself through persistent use of the
shift-response. The topic-shift is accomplished prematurely, before
the first speaker has had the opportunity to complete what he
regards as the full development of his subject. Yet it is accomplished without violation of the ritual obligations of responsiveness and occasions no blatant injuries of face.

PASSIVE PRACTICES

Passive practices constitute a more subtle expression of narcissism,
characterized not by the grabbing of attention but by miserliness
in the responses given to others. Such practices involve underutilization of the support responses that normally allow others to
pursue their topics. The effect is to let the other's topics die

through lack of encouragement, thereby opening the floor to the initiation of one's own topics.

To analyze the passive practices which recur most frequently, we must first distinguish between three different kinds of support-responses, which I call: *the background acknowledgment, the supportive assertion,* and *the supportive question. Background acknowledgments* are abbreviated responses such as "uh huh," "yeah," "oh really," and "umm." They are the weakest of the support-responses, but their use is important because they give the appearance that one is listening and wants the speaker to continue. *Supportive assertions* are complete declarative responses to the topic initiatives of others, and include evaluative statements ("I think that's great"), comments ("I never would have thought of him"), and suggestions ("You must see her right away"). A supportive assertion is a stronger response than the background acknowledgment, for it not only confirms that one is listening but indicates active engagement in the topic. *Supportive questions* are queries which draw out a speaker on his topic. They are the most encouraging of all support responses and the most active way of assuring that another's topic will be sustained.[12]

Passive practices involve *minimal use* and *differential use* of these three types of support-responses so that the topics of others are prematurely concluded. Minimal use contributes to the termination of a topic by withholding or delaying support-responses. Differential use means that a weaker support-response is chosen when a stronger one could be used.

Minimal use. Conversationalists cannot refrain from making any support-responses in the course of a conversation, as this would indicate too blatant an indifference to the other's topic.[13] Minimal use entails, then, a subtle unresponsiveness, where there is compliance with ritual expressions of attentiveness, but nevertheless a relative neglect of support-responses.

---

12. All support-responses are attention-giving responses which allow another conversationalist to hold the topical focus. I have characterized the "strength" of these responses in terms of how active a form of attention they suggest in the listener and how much support they provide for the other to remain as the focus of attention.

13. The absence of all such support-responses entitles the offended party to either inquire directly as to whether the other is listening or to directly express annoyance at the inattentiveness and to expect an apology.

The most devastating form is the avoidance of the supportive question. While not all topics depend on such questions for their perpetuation, a high percentage are carried, particularly in the early phases, by others' queries. While a topic can be aborted at any point by lack of interest, a lack of support and interest when it is first initiated most effectively kills it. One can speak of the take-off points or critical thresholds which shape the life-expectancy of the topic. If, in the first several turns of talk, the topic reaches take-off, it is far less vulnerable to derailment by minimal use. Prior to takeoff, topics die if they do not elicit either enthusiastic background acknowledgments or responsive questions which give explicit indication of support and interest. A string of supportive questions at the opening of a topic will normally guarantee a respectable life-expectancy for the topic, while the absence of any questions at this stage can be an ominous sign which signals premature termination.

Despite their importance, supportive questions are typically discretionary; under most circumstances, conversationalists are free to ask questions but are also at liberty not to. While there are certain initiatives which call for a mandatory response (if someone says, "I'm feeling so terrible," a supportive question like "What's wrong?" would normally be expected in return), most initiatives allow for far greater discretion. If John makes a topical initiative by saying, "I saw my friend Bill today," Jim can show active interest with a supportive question such as "How's he feeling?" or "How did it go?" He commits no offense, however, if he simply offers a background acknowledgment such as "hummm" or volunteers no support-response whatsoever.

Passive conversational narcissism entails neglect of supportive questions at all such discretionary points and extremely sparse use of them throughout conversation. Listening behavior takes place, but is passive. There is little attempt to draw others out or assume other forms of active listening. This creates doubt in the others regarding the interest of their topics or their rights to attention while, however, providing no clear basis for complaint about either inattentiveness or narcissism.

A second very common minimal-use practice involves the underutilization or delay of background acknowledgments. Although weaker than supportive questions, background acknowledgments such as "yeah" or "uh huh" are nonetheless critical cues by which speakers gauge the degree of interest in their topics. A variety of studies suggest that background acknowledgments facilitate the unfolding of topics and that their absence or delay can easily disrupt the development of the speaker's topic.[14]

Ritual restraints preclude withholding all background acknowledgments. Every conversationalist is expected to extend such minimal support even when he has no interest whatsoever in the topic.[15] Speakers can exploit this expectation by interjecting expressions such as "you know," subtle requests for immediate affirmations that indicate the other is paying attention. This is a way that conversationalists insecure about others' attention or interest can actively solicit support.

Despite the ritual constraints, there is sufficient freedom to permit a potent form of minimal response. While this can involve avoiding the background acknowledgment, it most often assumes the form of a delay in its insertion so that the speaker does not receive the immediate reinforcement that permits smooth continuation of his line of thought.[16] Studies have shown that background acknowledgments can be placed with precision timing and are often perfectly inserted during split-second pauses of the other's speech.[17] Conversationalists who delay their responses for

14. See especially Don H. Zimmerman and Candace West, "Sex Roles, Interruptions and Silences in Conversation," in Barrie Thorne and Nancy Henley (eds.), *Language and Sex*.

15. This leads to one of the most common deceptive practices in conversation, with the respondents mumbling "yeah" "uh huh" or other affirmations while paying only minimal attention and impatiently waiting to introduce their own concerns into the talk.

16. *Relative* discretion is permitted in frequency of use; conversationalists vary in the frequency with which they make background acknowledgments, both because of differences in personality and interactional style and in their characteristic responsiveness. It is worth noting that certain conversationalists who have strong need for validation may find their topics undermined not only by narcissistic others who extend relatively infrequent acknowledgments, but also others who may be responsive but whose conversational style does not involve frequent responses of this kind. Speakers who differ significantly in their use of background acknowledgments or other support-responses may find it difficult to talk to one another, not understanding the forms of validation which facilitate each other's speech.

17. See Gail Jefferson, "A Case of Precision Timing in Ordinary Conversation: Overlapped Tag-Positioned Address Terms in Closing Sequences," *Semiotica* (1969), pp. 48–96. See also Zimmerman and West, "Sex-Roles."

up to several seconds after another speaker has paused can throw him off-balance, disrupting his flow of speech and causing him to wonder whether his listeners are genuinely interested. Repetition of the delayed response creates more gaps in the rhythm, slowing the momentum of the conversation further and suggesting the need for a change in topic.[18] Such passive narcissism is rarely a conscious device to gain attention, but is nonetheless a common means by which self-oriented conversationalists "underrespond" to the topics of others and thus open the floor to their own.

Differential Use: Differential use involves the offering of the weakest support-response consistent with the demands of civility.[19] By exercising his discretion to select the least encouraging support-response, the self-oriented conversationalist hastens the termination of others' topics. This is often accomplished by the use of background acknowledgments where far stronger responses, especially a supportive question, might be more appropriate:

> *Mary:* Oh, I had the most awful headache all day.
> Tom was awful at work and, uh, just kept bothering
> me and bothering me. And Louise, too, more of the
> same. I'm so sick of it.
> *John:* Yeah.

In this instance, Mary has opened with a complaint calling for a stronger, more supportive response than the one offered. Typically, with such openings, a supportive question to draw out the speaker's feelings or experiences sets the stage for fully playing out the topic.[20] By substituting the minimal acknowledgment where a question could have been asked, John discourages Mary's initiative. She has the option to continue, but will find it difficult to do so in the face of repeated discouragement of this form.

---

18. The study by Zimmerman and West, "Sex-Roles," shows a linking of delayed response with premature topic termination and topic changeover, reporting that in at least three of ten transcripts topic closure follows regularly on the heels of a sequence of such repeated delayed responses.
19. Jessie Bernard uses the more general term "minimal response" to refer to what I have called differential use. Her notion of minimal response includes elements of my categories of minimal use as well as differential use. See Bernard, *The Sex Game,* especially Chapter 6.
20. A topic carried by questions is as follows:

Different conversationalists vary in their vulnerability to such discouragement, depending on their assertiveness, security, and other personality factors affecting their need for responsiveness from others. Those most vulnerable are those dependent on the strongest support-responses, on being drawn out through supportive questioning. Differential use will effectively silence these speakers. At the other extreme, the most aggressive conversationalists will pursue their topics even when their initiatives elicit only weak background acknowledgments or none at all. The only effective narcissistic practice with such speakers is an active one, through aggressive use of the shift-response in one's own behalf.

Successfully aborting others' topics does not always insure a turning of conversation to oneself, but, at minimum, prepares the stage for this possibility. At topic termination any speaker may seek to initiate his or her own topic. A second topic competition can then follow which may or may not reproduce the characteristics of the one just completed. In the pure narcissistic pattern, a conversationalist will act to discourage every topic and initiate continuing competition until he or she succeeds in securely establishing his or her own. In practice, few conversationalists remain unresponsive to *all* topics of others, but will exercise selective discretion, reinforcing with support-responses a limited number that are of interest and discouraging the others with minimal and differential use.

Mary: What a day at school.
John: What happened?
Mary: Oh, the kids were just impossible.
John: Was it Ann and Larry again?
Mary: Yeah, plus a few others. They were all . . .

Here a comparable topical initiative receives the stronger support-response and is brought to "takeoff" by repetition of supportive questions. The importance of the supportive question in securing the topic of others suggests why narcissistic practice involves a very low reliance on such questions.

Part II
Formal Dynamics

Power

*In front of, and defending, the larger political-economic structure
that determines our lives and defines the context of human relationships, there is a micropolitical structure that helps maintain it.
The "trivia" of everyday life—using "sir" or first name, touching
others, dropping the eyes, smiling, interrupting and so on   that
characterize these micropolitics are commonly understood as facil-
itators of social intercourse, but are not recognized as defenders
of the status quo—of the state, of the wealthy, of authority, of all
those whose power may be challenged. Nevertheless, these min-
utiae find their place on a continuum of social control which extends from internalized socialization (the colonization of the mind)
at the one end to sheer physical force (guns, clubs, incarceration)
at the other.*

NANCY HENLEY, *from "Power, Sex and
Nonverbal Communication"*

Introduction

In Part I we have seen that informal attention-dynamics in America are individualistic, with people tending to seek attention for themselves. There are, however, systematic differences between the sexes and among social classes that are aspects of "formal" behavior.[1] Of prime interest is the behavior of women and subordinate class members involving self-effacement and the giving of attention to others. In Part II, focusing mainly on formal rather than informal interactions, we examine sex roles and social class prescriptions which restrict "self-orientation" among lower-status groups and dictate a distribution of attention consistent with dominant social hierarchies.

In Part I we looked solely at informal interactions where people have the greatest freedom of individual initiative and are less strictly bound by the status and role requirements that govern their behavior in more structured areas. When we turn to formal interactions, as between doctor and patient, mother and infant, or employer and employee, it becomes apparent that the way people seek and give attention and the amount they are likely to receive is significantly shaped by their social roles and their status within the major institutional hierarchies. The analysis in Part II is fundamentally concerned with the link between face-to-face processes and social structure, focusing on the way that social roles define the responsibility for giving and getting attention in formal interactions (and to a lesser degree in informal conversation) according to gender and social class.

---

1. See pp. 3 ff for the definition of informal and formal behavior.

Allocating Attention in Formal Interactions

We must consider first the way that attention is allocated in formal interactions. In these interactions, which are organized to accomplish specific institutional purposes, individual initiative and individual responsibility are subject to the constraints of the institutional roles the individual is expected to perform. In the formal interaction within a classroom, for example, initiatives for attention are largely governed by the teacher and student roles, the teacher being required to take those initiatives necessary to teach in the institutionally approved manner and students expected to limit their own attention-getting initiatives in a manner dictated by the educational process.

The allocation system in formal interactions is thus one of "controlled" rather than "free" initiative, determined largely by the institutional roles. Such roles can be characterized as either attention-getting or attention-giving, depending on whether the actor is expected to give or get it. The teacher role is attention-getting while that of student is attention-giving; similarly, the role of the psychiatrist is attention-giving while that of his client is attention-getting. Those in attention-giving roles are expected to make primarily attention-giving rather than attention-getting initiatives and are thus restrained from the subtle egoism permitted in informal interaction.

ROLES AND STATUS: POWER AND THE ATTENTION-GETTING ROLE

The social allocation of attention-getting and attention-giving roles among different groups largely determines who gets attention in formal interactions. Individuals who typically take on attention-getting institutional roles learn to expect and seek attention for themselves, while those most often assigned attention-giving roles assume a certain socially imposed invisibility. In Part II I show, first, that the allocation of these roles is a function of power, with the great majority of attention-getting roles assigned to dominant groups and attention-giving roles to subordinate ones. I suggest that social dominance is institutionalized face-to-face through an organization of roles in families, workplaces, and politics which permits those of higher status to claim attention as their due and requires lower-status individuals to seek and accept less.

Groups that are expected to assume primarily attention-giving roles in formal interactions learn a generalized psychology that discourages focus on oneself and predisposes the individual to give attention in all phases of social life. Such an "attention-giving" psychology diverges significantly from the individualistic psychology encouraged more broadly in the culture and reflects variations in social character linked to status and dominance. Patriarchal and social class roles encourage the prevailing "self-orientation" most strongly among members of empowered groups, while fostering among women and other subordinate groups an "other-orientation" based on subordination of self and interactional deference. While I have focused in Part I only on the dominant self-oriented patterns, I explore in Part II different behaviors among those lacking power—ones of self-effacement and attention-giving closely institutionally regulated in formal settings and more subtly enforced in informal conversation.

INEQUALITY FACE-TO-FACE: ATTENTION AND SOCIAL STRUCTURE

Part II departs significantly from Part I because of its focus on formal interactions and its concern with institutionally-defined power; attention-processes were explored in Part I with reference to culture (individualism) while ignoring social structure. Part II introduces new themes of equality in face-to-face life and the link between interpersonal dynamics and socioeconomic power.

The concern with status differences will highlight the idea that attention is a unique face-to-face resource, allocated and distributed much like economic wealth. Attention can be understood as an interactional currency subject to distributive justice or inequity. Part II develops the thesis that social inequalities conceived in traditional social analysis as economic or political inequalities are also simultaneously "inequalities of face," institutionalized in interpersonal life and in a distribution of attention mirroring the allocation of other resources.

The inequalities of face are not simply interesting derivatives of economic and social power, but an integral dimension of their very structure. Stratification systems create distinctions of social worth that are communicated, learned, and enforced in ordinary face-to-face processes. One aspect of class hierarchy is that members of subordinate classes are regarded as less worthy of attention in relations with members of dominant classes and so are subjected to subtle but systematic face-to-face deprivations. The directing of attention to those defined by their class as "better" or more important lies at the very heart of class power as played out in everyday social relations and suggests a new vehicle for investigating the meaning of class itself.

The treatment of these problems requires certain shifts in the frame of analysis developed in Part I that deserve explicit emphasis. First, as already discussed, an examination of roles is introduced to demonstrate the way that face-to-face processes are organized according to the requirements of the dominant social structure. Second, while focusing only on the internal dynamics of interaction in Part I, I also consider in Part II the *access* of different groups to interactional settings in which they can expect attention. Members of dominant groups are privileged not only because face-to-face processes are internally structured to their advantage, but also because they have access to a greater range of interactional settings in which attention can normally be expected. A simple example is the greater capacity of the affluent to "purchase" attention by entering psychotherapy. The analysis in Part II is thus broadened to consider the diverse ways in which face-to-face dynamics interact with and reflect the larger societal context.

Chapter 3

The Gift of Attention-giving:
On Women Imposed

"Pray, what are you laughing at?", inquired the Rocket; "I am not laughing."
"I am laughing because I am happy," replied the Cracker.
"That is a very selfish reason," said the Rocket angrily. "What right have you to be happy? You should be thinking about others. In fact, you should be thinking about me. I am always thinking about myself, and I expect everybody else to do the same. That is what is called sympathy."

OSCAR WILDE, *from "The Remarkable Rocket"*

"Her voice was ever soft, gentle and low; an excellent thing in women."

SHAKESPEARE, *from* King Lear

Men and women learn to pursue attention differently and expect and accept it in different amounts.[1] In all patriarchal societies, women are typically assigned the attention-giving roles and men the attention-getting ones.[2] Accordingly, attention-giving becomes

---

1. These differences are most pronounced in formal interactions, but emerge in lesser degree in informal interactions as well. In this chapter we look first at formal interactions and then return to consideration of the informal interactions and conversations discussed in Part I.
2. Patriarchal societies have been defined as those in which economic, political, and cultural authority is exercised primarily by men. For general theoretical discussions of the patriarchal system, see Nancy Chodorow, *The Social Reproduction of Mothering,* and Steven Goldberg, *The Inevitability of Patriarchy.*

defined as a "feminine" skill and responsibility, with men gaining attention as a privilege of their gender.

Female Roles: Mother as Prototype

Betty Friedan, Jessie Bernard, and other students of sex roles have found that women's roles, public and private, mirror that of the mother. The mother role is the archetypical attention-giving one, in which women must give attention without expecting an equal measure in return. This is illustrated in the following account:

> Julie, about age five, picked up a child's book and began to look at the pictures while Mother read *Good Housekeeping*. Julie began showing pictures to her mother. In response, mother would look up either immediately or after a short pause, carefully look at the picture, question Julie about some aspect (e.g., "That's a sandwich?") and then comment or laugh amusedly about the book. Sometimes they would talk about Julie's experience with particular animals or kinds of food that she saw in the pictures.
>
> During this period, Mother showed interest in all of Julie's observations, giving Julie steady eye contact whenever Julie initiated these short conversations; in general, she communicated her interest in her daughter by listening and asking questions.
>
> Julie then put down her magazine and sat down on the bench beside her mother. She leaned her head against Mother's shoulder, put her arm around her back, and cuddled close while looking at Mother's magazine. Mother responded by leaning her head against her daughter's and pointing out pictures of interest. Eventually, however, she told Julie to remove her arm because it was bothering her. Julie complied without appearing offended, but remained snuggled close.
>
> Mother and daughter remained in this position for quite awhile. During this time mother showed increas-

ing irritation at Julie for pointing out pictures in the
magazine, for leaning too heavily against her, or for
showing impatience. Mother looked up at Julie less
frequently in response to her comments.

When Julie asked her mother who painted the wall,
mother crossly told her that no one had painted it,
that it was wallpaper. However, Julie did not modify
her comments and actions in response to her mother's
irritability. She still smiled much of the time and cud-
dled close.[3]

This observation dramatizes the child-centeredness of a typical
mother-child interaction and highlights how a mother must sur-
render the focus of attention. The daughter initiates and pursues
conversation about things she notices while the mother gives
attention by listening and drawing her out. At first, the mother
listens intently and responds with real interest. Her growing
impatience as the interaction proceeds, however, reflects the
attention-imbalance. Jessie Bernard has emphasized that in
America there are no clear limitations on how much attention a
mother is expected to give; in general, the "good" mother should
give as much as the child seems to require.[4]

We see here that a mother can, at minimum, expect some

---

3. This is the first of a series of observations of attention-dynamics in
everyday social interaction, taken from the Attention-Interaction Project
supervised by the author. For a description of the study, see the Intro
duction, pp. 7-8. All future illustrations, unless otherwise indicated, are drawn
from this study.

4. Bernard has stressed the extreme demands of the mother role in American
society, including the expectation of self-subordination and accommodation
of the attention-demands of the child. She describes the characteristic
interactional pattern:

> For perhaps an hour, the woman can maintain a degree of tranquility by
> centering all of her attention on the child. She tells stories. She plays
> games. She shares toys. She can meet the child's insatiable demands for
> attention with moderate ease. As time passes, however, this becomes
> harder and harder. As she shows signs of flagging, the demands of the
> child become more and more insistent. In her eagerness to placate the
> child's demands, she has been rewarding its distressing behavior.

See Jesse Bernard, *The Future of Motherhood,* p. 112-13.

reciprocal attention. Her child looks back at her, asks questions, and volunteers feelings. In addition, a mother does occasionally become the focus of the interaction, as when her child wants to know why she is feeling bad or seems upset.[5]

Since she has power over her child, a mother can also maintain some control over when she gives or withholds attention. In many other roles, however, women have less power to assert limits on their attention-giving. As wives or workers, for example, they are inferior in power to those they give attention and must normally defer to their demands.

As we have suggested, there is a close relation between the mother role and the other major female roles. In all the "female" occupational roles—nurse, child-care worker, secretary, social worker, domestic—some form of mothering is a primary interactional requirement. Similarly, a "good" wife is expected to nurture and support her husband and to be capable of unflagging attention, as with her child.

The distinctive feature of these roles is the expectation of attention-giving. The roles females assume that are attention-getting—such as movie actress or fashion model—are the exception and are available normally only to women deemed extraordinarily sexually attractive. In most of her roles and formal interactions, however, a woman assumes a certain invisibility. For example, studies of office interactions show that secretaries and receptionists are typically required to give a "motherly" focus to their bosses, which includes responding to their job-related or personal problems, while going subtly unattended themselves.[6] This pattern is also found in marriage and in child care, nursing, and other work roles.[7]

As described in Chapters 1 and 2, individualistic norms require people in ordinary informal interactions to assume responsibility

---

5. Children direct considerable attention to their mothers simply because they are the primary care-takers. This is suggestive of the fact that being in the role of attention-giver is the primary way that women get attention for themselves. Men, in contrast, gain attention without the obligation of assuming attention-giving roles and responsibilities.

6. See Mary Benet, *The Secretarial Ghetto*, p. 72 ff., and Jean Tepperman, *Not Servants, Not Machines; Office-Workers Speak Out*, Chapters 1-2.

7. See Jessie Bernard, *The Future of Marriage* and Louise Kapp Howe, *Pink Collar Workers*.

only for themselves and permit as much focus on oneself as can be successfully established in competition with others. However, women's roles stringently restrict such self-orientation (in their formal interactions). The mother prototype demands a non-individualistic attitude which includes responsibility for others. This differs radically from the expectations placed on males in their formal interactions and, as we shall see, reflects the inferior power of women in a patriarchy.

Male Roles: Attention and Patriarchal Power

Men in patriarchal societies are expected to assume relatively few attention-giving roles. While there are important variations, men in their formal interactions generally assume roles permitting them to concentrate on their own needs and to expect predominant attention in interactions with others, especially women.

The assignment of attention-getting roles to males is closely related to their societal power. Studies of small groups demonstrate a clear relation between power and attention-getting. Robert Bales and his followers at Harvard have shown that talking time and other measures of attention correlate strongly with measures of authority and leadership. "Task-leaders" of groups, who occupy authority roles like that of the traditional patriarchal father, speak far more than the other members and receive more eye contact and communication. Applying their research methods to the family, Bales and his associates have concluded that the father has tended to play the role of the "task-leader" in the American family and most often claims the attention associated with that role.[8]

The prototypical male role in Western societies has been the traditional patriarchal father. Novelistic and anecdotal accounts indicate that the classic patriarch exercised absolute control over family interaction. Oliver Wendell Holmes wryly characterized him as the "autocrat of the breakfast table." In the nineteenth century domicile, children and wife were expected to remain quiet unless

8. See especially Robert Bales, *Personality and Social Interaction* and Robert Bales and Talcott Parsons, *Family, Socialization and Interaction Process.*

questioned or otherwise directed to speak by the father or husband. Out of fear, power, and respect, the father commanded attention and focus whenever present in the family.

Despite the decline of absolute patriarchal authority, recent research suggests that the father's role remains one in which he can compel special forms of deference, support, and attention.[9] In my field studies of one hundred and fifty families, I found that fathers were interrupted less often when they spoke and were listened to with greater respect and patience. They also exercised greater control over the topics discussed and were more successful in gaining the focus of attention when they sought to do so. This pattern grows out of the father's institutional position and authority, as suggested in the observation below:

> The family is eating dinner. The father appears to have
> a very powerful position simply because of his status
> as "head of the family" and because he uses this status
> to exert veto power over what are legitimate topics of
> conversation and what are not. He very often silences
> his children when he considers their conversation to
> be frivolous or "not of general interest." Silencing is
> accomplished by short, angry statements. While he in-
> troduces subjects of conversation by making contro-
> versial and provocative statements, he never allows
> follow-up discussions which contradict his original
> statement. He virtually never contributes to or "ap-
> proves of" conversations which he does not initiate.

Here, the father dominates the interaction through aggressive assertion of his intellectual authority. As "head of household" and the bearer of higher status in the larger society, his ideas and statements carry special weight.[10] His children, sensitive to differ-

---

9. This research has been reviewed recently by Jessie Bernard. Based on studies of family interactions and statistics of mental and physical health, Bernard makes a compelling argument that the family provides superior support functions for the husband and is characterized by interactional patterns reflecting male power. See Bernard, *Future of Marriage.*

10. The importance of the father's status outside the family in shaping attention-dynamics within it is suggested further by this report from an observer of attention-dynamics within his own family:

ences in power, respond to his words both because of his authority in the family and his knowledge and experience in the larger world.

A wife also learns to defer to her husband's higher status. Observers of husband-wife interactions reported that the wife gave more supportive responses and active encouragement to her husband's talk about himself, while the husband listened less well and was less likely to actively "bring her out" about herself and her own topics.[11] This suggests perpetuation of the traditional family roles in which males provide economic support in return for wifely attention and deference.

As in the family, men occupy the predominant attention-getting roles in the larger society. These include managerial roles such as politician and corporate executive, as well as the major professional roles such as doctor, lawyer, and university professor. All of these roles permit men to concentrate on themselves and to claim the focus of attention in their official interactions. They are roles in which the male typically has a coterie of attention-giving subordinates characteristically female—who attend to his personal and job needs. Furthermore, they are roles whose symbolic value compel deference and respectful attention from clients and patients in work interaction.[12]

It must be noted that the roles of men in work and public life differ considerably depending on their social class. Men who are not in the dominant classes do not enter the privileged attention getting roles and cannot typically expect attention or deference in work relations.[13] However, the roles of most male workers differ

---

My father is undoubtedly the most powerful in this respect. He is a professional with a national reputation and the subtle aura of his authority in the academic world is felt at home. I have always been conscious of the respect he receives from his colleagues and I greatly admire his opinion on everything. The source of his power and attention in the family lies in his credibility. He is always right.

11. From the Attention-Interaction Project. See pp. 7 ff.

12. These roles are examined at length in the next chapter. Some of these roles, such as doctor, carry with them expectations of attention-giving toward clients or patients. It will be shown that many of the attention-giving responsibilities are being removed from the professional's role and delegated to subordinates, who are typically female.

13. The exception is in the exchange of attention with other workers, explored on pp. 78 ff in the next chapter.

considerably from that of female workers because they require attention to machines or objects rather than people. The exceptions are such roles as staff aide or administrative assistant, which require an extreme personal attentiveness typically expected of females. Men in these positions must develop their capacities for giving attention more than other men and, like male secretaries or nurses, may experience contradictions between their work roles and their other male roles.

Attention and Character

Because women's roles are so different from men's, women are socialized to a particular psychology—one of attention-giving. In patriarchal cultures, females develop a social character of "other-orientation," which includes the attention-giving psychology, whereas males are socialized to the character type of "self-orientation," which entails an attention-getting psychology.[14] While recent social changes encourage greater self-orientation among women, sexual socialization continues to emphasize an other-oriented model for the female personality and encourages an attention-giving psychology among women that "fits" their typical roles. An analysis of male and female character can illuminate further the special interactional responsibilities placed on women and the formal restrictions on their rights to seek attention for themselves.

FEMALE CHARACTER: OTHER-ORIENTATION AND ATTENTION-GIVING

The idea that the socialized female character is "other-oriented" has been developed by many feminist writers, most notably Simone de Beauvoir. In *The Second Sex,* de Beauvoir distinguishes between the female mode of "being-for-the-other" and the male one of "being-for-the-self." An other-oriented person focuses on

---

14. See Chapter 2 (pp. 21 ff) for a discussion of the concept of a psychology of attention, including a definition of the "attention-giving" and "attention-getting" psychologies.

the needs, concerns, and interests of others; the primary concern, face-to-face, is to accommodate and affirm them. In contrast, the self-oriented person concentrates primarily on himself and his own well-being; face-to-face, he seeks attention for himself.

The "feminine" traits—sensitivity, warmth, sweetness, generosity, supportiveness, and responsiveness—are all expressions of other-orientation. In developing these qualities as part of their sexual identity and socialization, women acquire the basic elements of an attention-giving psychology. The sensitive and supportive "feminine" personality develops an unusual capacity to give nurturant attention for sustained periods of time. She learns to listen and share attention rather than seek it exclusively for herself.

This other-orientation is built on self-sacrifice, and a requirement of underplaying her own needs in everyday interactions. Accordingly, women learn not only to give attention to others, but experience some degree of doubt, fear, or guilt when taking it or accepting it for themselves. Mary Rohman, in an unpublished study based on tape-recordings of women talking with each other about conversation, reported that many of the women interviewed admitted to seeking invisibility or a low profile in social interactions, particularly in conversations with men. Some feel they simply do not deserve attention, while others indicated that their socialization has led them to feel less feminine when they compete to bring attention to themselves.[15]

Rohman's findings suggest that the other-oriented woman is doubly disadvantaged psychologically. First, she must struggle with underlying doubts about her own rights to attention. Many females, from an early age, experience anxiety and guilt even in the simplest acts of asserting themselves for attention:

> Even as a child I was afraid to compete for attention
> with my peers. As a child I was very invested in maintaining
> an image of gentle quietude, which I believe must have
> been forty percent fear. Learning to break through the
> quietude and passivity requires an act of faith and a cer-

15. Mary Rohman, "Conversations: Male and Female Experience" (including transcripts and analysis).

tain amount of reassurance that it will be worth the discomfort . . . [16]

Second, a woman's fears and doubts about taking attention are often linked to anxieties about femininity. A woman is in the unique position of having her sexual identity tied to the giving of attention. By giving it she validates her own femininity, not only in the eyes of males, who expect this behavior from her and reward her for it, but also frequently in her own eyes.

However, by seeking and taking attention, she can cast into doubt her feminine identity. If she competes aggressively with males, refusing to accept the expected attention-giving role, they may reject her sexually. Rohman quotes one woman as saying, "If I don't talk, it's because I know that a lot of the men will like me better for sexual kinds of reasons." Under these conditions, it may be easier for a woman to concede many of her own attention needs rather than place her sexual identity constantly in jeopardy.

Many women develop a specifically other-oriented way of seeking attention as a compromise between their needs for attention and their fear of demanding it directly. This is illustrated by one woman's description of how she learned to gain some attention in an encounter group:

> I had spent most of the time observing and watching
> other people run the group. They seemed to have a definite
> ideal of what was happening and I certainly didn't, so I
> wasn't able to compete for attention in that area. I
> finally found my own attention device, although when
> I began to talk I felt extremely embarrassed and I could
> hear my voice shaking. I spoke about some changes in
> my own feelings about the group, but I spoke in terms
> of the entire group, rather than confining the observa-
> tion to myself. It was a genuine observation—the first
> major one about the emotional state of the group it-
> self—but it also served the purpose of drawing a distinct

---

16. Drawn from preliminary interviews by the author of observers selected for the Attention-Interaction Project. In the process of their training, observers were interviewed regarding their own modes of giving and getting attention.

form of attention to myself. The group leader picked
up on the generalization immediately and attempted to
have me focus the observation back on myself. I felt
that he had somehow seen through me and could tell
that my good (encounter group) girl pose was no more
than a ploy for attention.[17]

This nicely illustrates the other-oriented model of seeking
attention. Attention is drawn indirectly to the self by speaking
about others. The woman here gets visual attention by talking,
while diverting topical attention to the group as a whole. Many
women gain attention by talking about those with whom they are
conversing (their children, husbands, etc.), thus winning attention
while simultaneously focusing on others.

MALE CHARACTER: SELF-ORIENTATION AND ATTENTION-GETTING

Turning to male psychology, we find again a "fit" between social
roles and character structure. The common male roles are attention-getting, encouraging the self-orientation central in American society. Two attributes of male psychology are (1) expecting
in everyday interactions to be a focus of attention, and (2) being
unable or unwilling to give more than civil attention.[18] These are
ordinary, taken-for-granted attitudes reflecting subtle male
privilege and power. Males are not openly taught that their sex
entitles them to special claims to attention; in fact, they are more
likely to be given instruction in the civilities of attending
courteously and graciously to others, particularly to women. Yet
this largely involves conformity to the ritual codes of civil
attention and male chivalry and does not conflict with broader
male self-orientation.

Just as women can validate their femininity by giving attention,
men can affirm their feelings of masculinity by actively pursuing

17. From an interview with the author in the Attention-Interaction Project.
18. Philip Slater's work on the relation between narcissism and sexual
identity is extremely useful in understanding the psychological characteristics
of the self-oriented male. See Slater, "Culture, Sexuality, and Narcissism," in
*Footholds: Understanding the Shifting Family and Sexual Tensions in Our
Culture.*

it. Males are generally socialized to a personality model that enables them to dominate attention; all the central masculine traits—aggressiveness, assertiveness, competitiveness, authoritativeness, self-assurance—are instrumental in gaining and maintaining attention. The following observation shows how "masculine" competitiveness and aggressiveness is advantageous in gaining attention in conversation:

> A man and a woman are sitting together at the bar intently absorbed in conversation. They both appear to be dynamic personalities, but he is more forceful and aggressive. He is doing most of the talking, most of it about himself; she does not appear resigned to the passive listening role and makes active efforts to enter the conversation. However, whenever they begin to talk at the same time, he persists aggressively, while she backs off. She makes no audible protest, but there is a flash of distress in her eyes each time this happens. On one occasion, she perseveres a little longer than usual, but he refuses to give way. He gives no sign he is aware she is trying to talk and simply raises his voice so it can be heard clearly over hers. Again, she sinks back silently in submission.

"Masculine" aggressiveness is here well adapted to the norms of individual initiative governing conversational attention.[19] Males are less bound than females by constraints on egoistic, self-assertive, or competitive behavior, and so are free to take the kind of forceful initiative that can silence others, especially women. Their aggressiveness is often linked to self-assurance and authoritativeness, equally important in winning attention:

> A mixed group of six people are sitting and talking at a table in a restaurant. The person at the "top" of the attention-hierarchy is a man who is outgoing and sure of himself. He maintains eye contact with everyone talking to him, initiates conversations in which he knows a lot about the subject, and appears to know more

---

19. See Chapter 1 for a review of the individual initiative system.

about any subject brought up than anyone else in the group. He sustains his dominance by using words like "definitely," "I'm sure of it," and "It's got to be that way because . . ." in a strong, sure tone of voice.[20]

Observers reported that males more frequently expressed themselves in this authoritative and assured manner, while females, often speaking in a hesitant or questioning tone of voice, were more likely to lose attention by showing uncertainty and lack of confidence.[21] This contrast reflects the underlying differences in socialized male and female character. Authoritativeness and self-assurance are central to the idealized masculine personality and are developed in boys through identification with cultural models of masculinity (such figures as John Wayne and Humphrey Bogart) and through traditional patterns of male socialization.[22]

Many males who are passive, quiet, or shy, while superficially less demanding of attention in ordinary interactions and less adequately equipped psychologically to claim it, have, nonetheless, been socialized to expect focal attention from women. Lacking the personal power to enforce their demands, they must rely more heavily on their public status or occupational position to secure attention. These men often impose an extra burden on women, as they expect no less attention than other males, but demand that women play a more active role in assuring that they get it.[23]

---

20. From the Attention-Interaction Project.
21. From the Attention-Interaction Project. These differences have been reported in other studies as well. See in Barrie Thorne and Nancy Henley (eds.), *Language and Sex*, especially the essay by Thorne and Henley, "Difference and Dominance: An Overview of Language, Gender and Society," pp. 5-42.
22. See, for example, Myron Brenton, *The American Male.*
23. This is not to minimize the plight of those less able than most men to live up to the ideal of the masculine personality. Many gentle, unaggressive, or "feminine" men are subject to severe face-to-face punitive treatment, often at the hands of women as well as other men. In winning attention, they are in many respects more disadvantaged than women because they have less social license to use "feminine" traits, such as emotionality or dependency. Thus, while some of these men hope to receive male privileges of attention, many do not succeed.

Informal Interactions: Conversation Between the Sexes

One can ask at this point whether the male attention-getting orientation and the female attention-giving orientation are expressed not only in formal interactions defined by their institutional roles but also in informal conversation in personal life. In Part I, we treated informal social life as a sphere in which social identities, inequalities, and roles are suspended and a pretence of equality among the participants is maintained. Were this strictly true, it would mean that men and women in many ordinary conversations are released from normal attention-getting and attention-giving expectations.

The restrictions on females taking attention and the assurances of males getting it are indeed far weaker in informal conversation than in formal interactions. Many women, by virtue of talkativeness, expressiveness, or emotional charisma, receive much attention in informal conversations and, unless they are extraordinarily domineering and competitive, do not face the same penalties they would elsewhere. Many women routinely compete over topics and display "conversational narcissism." Since this is the dominant American norm for informal behavior, women who constantly redirect the talk and attention to themselves do not necessarily experience the guilt, anxiety, or sense of threat to their femininity that constrains them in their formal interactions.

However, studies of everyday conversation suggest that the typical sex-role expectations are not completely suspended in informal social life. While status inequalities are less emphasised, people do not talk as socially neutral participants but as male and female conversationalists with different psychologies and different external constraints.[24] While women are permitted in informal conversations to be far more self-oriented than in their institutional roles, attention-giving is still defined mainly as a female responsibility and men are favored when competing for attention.

Support for this thesis comes from studies of the relative talking time in mixed groups, the topics most commonly discussed,

24. As indicated earlier (p. 10), "formal" attention-dynamics play an important part in informal interaction. The different expectations assigned to men and women in informal conversation are the most important example.

patterns of interruption and deference, and the relative responsive-ness of each sex to the other's ideas, feelings, and assertions. Studies of talking time do not sustain stereotypes of the "talkative female" and the "silent male." They indicate that men tend to speak more often and for longer periods of time, while women more frequently take the listening role.[25] (This has led feminists to suggest that the "talkative woman" is simply one who talks as much as a man.) Mary Rohman, in the study mentioned earlier, reports that many women say they are intimidated in male-female conversation, and feel powerless to control the flow of conversa-tion in groups of friends. Jessie Bernard, in reviewing anecdotal and available research evidence, concludes that it is somewhat unusual in a group for males to sit quietly and listen to females talking, while the reverse is much more common.[26]

Men are also more likely to control topics. Male-female con-versation is more likely to focus on "male" topics, whether they be personal topics about the individual male speakers or more impersonal topics like sports, cars, or politics.[27] "Female" topics, including children, clothes, or emotions, are reserved for conversations among women.[28]

As suggested in the last chapter, most ordinary conversation is ego-centered, the topics having something to do with one or another of the conversationalists. While it is conventional wisdom, enshrined in etiquette books and popular advice columns, that it is the male prerogative to talk about himself and the responsibility of the woman to draw him out,[29] empirical studies suggest a more complex process takes place. In my study of dinner conversations

25. The principal studies are those by William Soskin and Fred Hilpert, based on observations of male-female conversations in everyday life and in experi-mental laboratory settings. Both report patterns of greater talkativeness among men. See William Soskin and Vara John, "The Study of Spontaneous Talk," in Roger Barker (ed.) *The Stream of Behavior*, and Fred Hilpert, Cheris Kramer and Ruth Ann Clark, "Participants' Perceptions of Self and Partner in Mixed-Sex Dyads,"
26. See Bernard, "Talk, Conversation, Listening, Silence," in Bernard, *The Sex Game*, Chapter 6, and Rohman, "Conversations."
27. See Barrie Thorne, "Women in the Draft Resistance Movement," p. 268.
28. Ibid.
29. *The New Seventeen Book of Young Living* instructs girls to "concentrate on the other person. Ask questions to draw him out. He'll love talking about himself."

I found that a substantial majority of the topics initiated by conversationalists were about themselves, with no significant differences in this regard between men and women.[30] However, other research suggests that females are more likely to be responsive to male initiatives, while males frequently respond in ways that undermine women's efforts to talk about themselves.[31] Men are particularly inclined to react with what I have called "minimal response" (see Chapter 1), a response that is not blatantly rude, but so small (such as "hmmm") as to induce doubt in the other about one's attention. Speaking up and pursuing their own topic is thus a greater risk for women, who often face the unpleasant choice of either remaining quiet or talking and feeling foolish or anxious about whether anyone is really listening.[32]

There is preliminary evidence that support-responses, responses that encourage the topics of others and do not cause a shift in attention back to the self, are sex-linked. In studies of dinner conversations I found that women are more likely to ask supportive questions. Drawing others out is a special skill associated with nurturance and mothering. It is also part of a feminine style which holds and attracts men. Most conversational studies suggest that listening is an essentially female skill. While listening is socially necessary, it is not generally rewarded in an individualistic, self-oriented culture. Women are expected to listen because of their subordinate status.[33] Given the prevailing culture, it is

---

30. See p. 8.
31. See Don Zimmerman and Candace West, "Sex-Roles, Interruptions and Silences in Conversation," in Thorne and Henley (eds.), *Language and Sex,* and Bernard, "Talk, Conversation."
32. This puts in a new perspective the stereotype of the tongue-wagging woman who talks incessantly, even when no one is listening. Male unresponsiveness means that women must learn to talk with less support or feedback. They must, in a sense, tune out unresponsiveness, either by ignoring it or by becoming invulnerable to it. Otherwise, they will be paralyzed.
33. Males are not only less supportive of female topics but are more aggressive as competitors for their own topics. This suggests that shift-responses (see p. 23) are also sex-linked. Interruptions, for example, a major form of shift-response, are a male prerogative. Zimmerman and West have shown, in a study of conversations recorded in coffee shops, drug stores, and other public places, that while males frequently interrupt females, the reverse is a relatively rare occurence. According to the authors, this is linked to a generalized male privilege in abruptly turning talk to his own topics and

scarcely surprising that even many women violate these expectations; yet many others do learn to listen and these are held up as
models for feminine behavior.

Nonetheless, women are free in many conversations to assume
the talking role as well. Since male needs for attention are better
met in their work and family roles, they are willing to cede women
a certain measure of attention in sociability, where it costs them
little and allows females to feel they are not being totally
neglected. Women, on the other hand, cannot approach conversation so casually. The common opinion that women have a greater
need to socialize and to talk reflects their greater attention
deprivation in their institutional roles; women depend heavily on
conversation as a compensatory arena. Extremely verbose women,
who alienate others by talking constantly, have turned to the
"proper" domain for attention, but are unable to contain themselves within the prescribed latitudes.

As indicated earlier, even when women talk, it is often in ways
that steer attention to others rather than themselves. As part of
their other-orientation many women learn to feel a responsibility
for the feelings of others in conversation and so act in ways that
promote others' sense of well-being and security. Women talk to
smooth over awkward silences, to ease latent conflicts, to make
others feel at home, and to include people who are not being
noticed. Moreover, a woman will often speak only when she senses
a man does not wish to talk himself and wants her to take up the
slack. She may quickly retreat when she receives a signal that he is
ready to begin speaking.

Even when women seek attention for themselves by talking,
talkativeness itself does not guarantee success. Patterns of ritu-
alistic listening described in the last chapter, associated with nods
of the head or minimal acknowledgments while thoughts are far
from the conversation, is a common means by which males
succeed in denying attention to talkative women. In families,
talkative mothers are often "tuned out" by other family members.

---

interests (Zimmerman and West, "Sex-Roles"). My analysis of dinner conversations suggested that while both men and women make abundant use of
the shift-response to redirect talk to themselves, males do this more blatantly
and display less sensitivity to the needs of women to complete their topics.

The family is at dinner and the mother is talking all the
time. She is talking mostly about her organizational work—
what her current projects are and how they are coming
along. She then begins talking about what she and her
girlfriend from out of town did during the day. Everybody continued to eat and seemed, at best, to be listening half-heartedly. Occasionally, one of the others at the
table would pop up with a question, almost as though it
was required to show some sign of interest. While the
mother talked, all the others looked down and were
giving most of their attention to what was on their
plates.

One of the most common complaints of wives is the reluctance
of their husbands—lost behind their breakfast newspapers or their
own internal preoccupations—to listen. Female talkativeness is
often a response to male withdrawal and uncommunicativeness,
creating a deteriorating cycle in which her increased talk leads
only to being more ignored.

Under certain circumstances, normally involving either flirtation
and sexuality or female helplessness and dependency, men do
listen and accord women the attention-getting position. Girls learn
early that males will give them attention on the basis of sexual
interest, and so learn to connect attention and sexuality far more
closely than boys. Many come to believe that their sexuality is
their most legitimate claim on attention and learn to view
attention as a reward for pleasing men physically. This is reinforced by male attention-giving in conversation, which can vary
erratically depending on sexual interest. Men who typically refuse
the listening role often become highly attentive and conversa-
tionally responsive to women who are attractive to them. At the
same time, they are likely to withdraw their attention and again
focus on themselves when their sexual interests change or decline.
This leaves women at the mercy of sexual dynamics which are
often subterranean, but create bizarre and disturbing shifts in the
attention they receive. When a man gives a woman attention—even
by listening attentively—she must, in many situations, immediately
wonder whether he has sexual expectations; if he obviously does,
she can feel comfortable taking more attention only if she expects
to be sexually responsive. Women must constantly reassess the

situation and consider whether by accepting attention from men they are consenting—or appearing to consent—to a hidden agenda that is not their own.

Being attentive and responsive to women who attract them sexually is one of the few forms of attention-giving in which men do not compromise their masculinity. While they are temporarily relinquishing their attention-getting prerogatives, they remain self-oriented and expect sexual rewards in return. Moreover, when a man affirms a woman in her sexuality, he is implicitly affirming his own sexuality, one of the few occasions in which the self-oriented male behaves with the recognition that affirmation of the other can be a way of affirming the self.

When sexuality is not a factor, men are most likely to accept a listening role if a woman presents herself as weak or helpless. The therapeutic model, in which a strong male gives attention to a weak female, extends beyond therapy to ordinary conversation. Men assume uncharacteristic listening postures toward women who send clear signals of vulnerability and distress. This kind of male attention stems from the chivalrous and patriarchal code that dictates masculine protection for a feminity that acknowledges its own dependency.

In therapy, the person who receives attention is less "power-ful." This unusual separation of power and attention generally characterizes the circumstances under which men give attention to women. Unlike women, men do not normally give attention from a position of weakness or social inferiority but only when their own strength and power is being reaffirmed. This suggests why crying and other expressions of emotional distress are especially effective female ways of getting attention. A woman's tears are not only an open acknowledgment of her vulnerability, but a seductive invitation for the male to assume the position of strength that validates his masculinity.

This points to one of the few competitive advantages that women exercise in attention-getting. Although attention is not allocated according to need,[34] openly expressing need can be a powerful means of claiming it. The rules of civility described in the last chapter require that attention be given to those obviously

34. See Chapter 1 for discussion of this point.

in distress—and most people do respond in such cases, either out of politeness or genuine compassion. The greater freedom of women to cry, show vulnerability, or acknowledge helplessness is, other than sexuality, their strongest claim on attention.

The expectation that men do not cry or show their feelings is one of the most significant impediments to males getting attention. This is particularly the case for men socialized to a strict model of masculinity in which any expression of feeling is regarded as self-indulgent, and any betrayal of need or insufficiency as effeminate. Such men are committed to an image of strength and self-control that can be easily interpreted as a disavowal of any need for attention, and can discourage others from giving any they might otherwise be inclined to offer.

For some men, the requirements of masculinity lead not only to inhibition of weeping, but also inability to open up about personal difficulties, or even to talk about themselves at all. Such males frequently assume the role of therapist in their personal conversations, becoming uncommonly good listeners with women, but at the same time maintaining their sense of masculinity by identifying with the power of the therapist's role. However, the pretence that they have no needs and are fully in control of themselves can lead to a subtle form of attention-deprivation. Such men may share the subtle sense of oppression experienced by many women that they are constantly listening to the other sex without any real reciprocation.

Many men envy the female freedom to be openly emotional and vulnerable, and covet the kind of attention it brings. Feminine emotionality, however, gives women only a limited advantage in claiming attention. As in the case of children, it is easily disparaged as "infantile" and used as a pretext for denying women attention. Except in special settings, women must generally limit their emotionality in social interactions in order to be taken seriously. Moreover, men, while handicapped by their lack of emotional expressiveness, can rely on the socialized skill of women to intuit and be responsive to their unacknowledged feelings and needs.

Chapter 4

Attention for Sale:
The Hidden Privileges of Class

**[This chapter was co-authored with
Dr. Yale Magrass.]**

*Suddenly, a sharp, dry cough was heard, and they all looked
around. It came from a tall supercilious looking Rocket, who was
tied to the end of a long stick. He always coughed before he made
any observation, so as to attract attention.*
*"Ahem, Ahem," he said, and everybody listened . . . As soon as
there was perfect silence, the Rocket coughed a third time and
began. He spoke with a very slow distinct voice, as if he was
dictating his memoirs, and always looked over the shoulder of
the person to whom he was talking. In fact, he had a most distinguished manner. "I am a very remarkable Rocket, and come of
remarkable parents. My mother was the most celebrated Catherine
Wheel of her day, and was renowned for her graceful dancing.
When she made her public appearance she spun around nineteen
times before she went out and each time that she did so she threw
into the air seven pink starts. My father was a Rocket like myself
and of French extraction. He flew so high people were afraid that
he would never come down. He did though, for he was of a kindly
disposition, and he made a most brilliant descent in a shower of
golden rain . . ."*
*"I am made for public life" said the Rocket, "and so are all my
relations . . . Whenever we appear we excite great attention . . ."*

OSCAR WILDE, from "The Remarkable Rocket"

*A high-school girl who detectives say wanted to put some zest in
her life was charged with second-degree forgery yesterday in the
theft of about $32,000 from her parents' savings accounts. De-
tectives said Sandra Lee Smart, 19, of Boulder, bought a new
Thunderbird, Jaguar and a $25,000 Lincoln Continental to be-*

*come popular and change her humdrum life-style. "She told me
she knew she would be caught sooner or later, but it was worth
it," said detective Steve Dillman. "She got people to notice her . . ."*

THE BOSTON GLOBE, November 30, 1978 (UPI)

*What is at issue here, however, is the question: how far is com-
modity exchange together with its structural consequences able
to influence the* total *outer and inner life of society?*

GEORG LUKACS, from *History and Class-Consciousness*

We have seen in the last chapter a close relation between attention
and power. In America, wealth, occupation, and education all
significantly affect who gets attention in everyday interactions,
with members of privileged groups receiving the most and those in
subordinate groups experiencing a certain daily invisibility.
Inequalities of attention grow out of the most fundamental forms
of social inequality and must be understood partly as a feature of
a society divided into classes.

Socially dominant classes have the power to define themselves
as having greater personal and social worth than those in inferior
positions and thus more deserving of attention. They are best able
to exhibit the prevailing societal symbols of worth, symbols
described by Richard Sennett as "badges of ability" that all
members of society accept as tangible measures of merit. By
displaying these symbols, people affirm themselves in the eyes of
others as individuals of special distinction, whose abilities and
achievements give them unqualified claim to attention.[1] In strati-
fied societies, dominant classes largely define these symbols and
assign them to achievements and possessions reflecting their own
class advantages.

In America, the dominant classes are those which come to
control economic, political, and cultural life. They include the
monied class that owns economic resources and the emerging class
of managers and professionals that exercises economic and cultural
authority over the rest of the population. The subordinate classes

---

1. See Richard Sennett and Jonathan Cobb, *The Hidden Injuries of Class.*

include a marginal underclass comprising the poor, unemployed, and peripherally employed, and the working class whose members are employed, but do not own capital or exercise authority.[2] Members of dominant classes have advantages in gaining attention in what we have called "formal" interactions principally because of their power and official status.[3] They monopolize the commanding attention-getting roles in cultural and political life and in workplaces. In addition, they are advantaged in informal interactions because wealth, occupation, and education create added claims to attention in ordinary conversations. We shall begin by considering the relation of attention to wealth—first in formal, then in informal interactions—and then consider how occupational roles and educational standing affect the attention any individual receives.

Attention as a Commodity: Wealth and the Purchase of Attention

In modern industrial societies, a growing percentage of the individual's social life occurs in "secondary" relationships mediated by money and commercial interests. People must seek to satisfy their basic needs—including attention—in interactions

---

2. The working class, as understood here, includes blue-collar and many white-collar and service workers who are often characterized as "middle class" in popular discourse. The characterization of "middle class" obscures the fact that these workers, many of whom are moderately well paid, do not exercise control over their work or cultural institutions and are subject to the authority of capital and the professional-managerial class. The dominant classes, as understood here, refer to those popularly referred to as the "upper class" and the "upper-middle" class and comprise at most between twenty and thirty percent of the population.

3. Formal interactions are those strictly regulated by institutional roles and purposes. The system for the allocation of attention in formal interactions, based on the organization of attention-getting and attention giving roles, is described on pp. 40 ff. In the analysis of formal interactions and their relation to class, we are concerned, as indicated earlier, not only with how attention is allocated *within* given interactions, but with the different *access* of members of different groups to formal settings and interactional roles in which they can normally expect attention. We thus explore here both "class" dynamics internal to interactions and the class character of the larger social structure in which attention-getting roles are allocated mainly to privileged groups. For a discussion of this approach, see pp. 41 ff, in the Introduction to Part II.

governed directly or indirectly by the market. Attention has become increasingly available as a commodity to be purchased from people who give attention in the course of their work and expect to be paid for their services. Members of the dominant classes are best able to afford attention of this kind and consume the greatest amount.

Consider, for example, the purchase of attention in psychotherapy. Therapy is a market-based formal interaction explicitly structured to assure the client-purchaser most of the attention. In exchange for a fee, the client is assured that the only legitimate focus or "subject" of the interaction is herself. (The therapist who repeatedly seeks to introduce himself as the focus of attention violates the most fundamental norm of therapy). The therapist is the quintessential professional attention-giver, for the focus of his training is the development of attention-giving skills and it is these skills for which he is paid.

In the therapeutic setting, unlike many other market settings, there is no subtlety cloaking the exchange of attention for money, as the therapist publicly offers his attention and the client openly purchases it. In the therapeutic process itself, however, the therapist must convince his client that he is giving his attention out of genuine concern and sympathy rather than for purely pecuniary ends or the therapeutic endeavor is likely to fail. This reflects the fact that people are most gratified by attention they believe others spontaneously choose to give. Thus, even people purchasing attention want to believe that the other is giving his attention freely rather than because his purchase requires it.

Psychoanalysis and psychotherapy continue to be a luxury enjoyed by business and professional classes. Members of subordinate classes can rarely afford to enter psychotherapy and so must seek other, and less expensive, forms of attention. The options are limited, however, as access to most of the attention-getting roles (and formal interactions) in the marketplace requires considerable money, and those roles which they may be able to afford offer less attention than those available to the privileged.

The purchase of attention in restaurants, a very different kind of market setting, illustrates this point well. Getting attention is part of the pleasure of "eating out," even in a modest restaurant where the amount of attention the customer can normally expect is limited to the simple serving of a meal.[4]

But the attention purchased in the expensive restaurant is distinct. The reputation of an exclusive restaurant rests not only in the quality of its food, but its capacity to deliver in delicately-structured interactions the extra attention for which its affluent clientele is presumably deserving and able to pay ~~for~~. Consider the following observation:

> We were greeted by the owner himself, who was dressed
> in extremely formal attire, but welcomed us informally,
> as if he were personally pleased to see us. All through the
> meal, one waiter hovered over our table watching to see
> if we needed anything. He moved quickly to fill our
> glasses and to make sure that we had the right sauces
> and condiments. The head waiter had a distinguished
> manner, with the expected French accent, and was ex-
> tremely deferential. In taking our orders, he spoke softly
> and unobtrusively, yielding the floor immediately when-
> ever one of us began to speak. He was responsive to our
> inquiries, showing considerable knowledge of gastronomy,
> but careful not to draw too much attention to himself.
> He listened solicitously to each person's order, nodding

---

4. In considering formal interactions in settings such as restaurants, we must distinguish between "focused" and "partly focused" kinds of interactions (pp. 11 ff). "Focused" interaction between waiter and customer occurs whenever they are directly engaged in talk, as when the customer is ordering the food or the waiter inquires how good it tastes. In these interactions, the shared cognitive focus of attention is clearly on the customer, as it is his food, comfort, and needs that are the subject or topic of the interaction and constitute the focus of awareness of both parties in the interaction.

"Partly focused" interaction also occurs between waiter and customer. Goffman has described partly focused interaction as that where there are persons officially present in the situation who are excluded from participation in the interaction. This defines the situation of the waiter at the stage when the meal is being eaten; he is expected to remain discreetly attentive to his customers without taking part in their talk among themselves. Such "partly focused" attention is an important form purchased by customers or clients in other settings as well, for example, from sales personnel in boutiques or department stores or from attending nurses in hospitals. See Erving Goffman, *Behavior in Public Places*, pp. 91ff.

supportively or appreciatively at the selections and
never allowing his gaze to wander. All staff members
were, in fact, extremely attentive. The wine stewards,
busboys, and waiters also approached us respectfully
and served the food with a sense of exquisitely con-
centrated care and concern.[5]

Here, the role of customer is a source of exceptional attention.
The patron purchases the services of a variety of attention-givers,
as well as the rights to a carefully cultivated face-to-face deference.
He can immediately engage those serving him[6] and, in face-to-face
interaction, can expect unhurried and uninterrupted attention.
These waiters[7] are trained to give undivided visual attention, to
listen solicitously, and to refrain from making themselves the

---

5. From the Attention-Interaction Project supervised by the author. All
examples cited henceforth in this chapter are drawn from this research, unless
otherwise specified. This particular report is one of a small number based on
participant-observation.

6. An important "privilege" of attention involves the conditions under which
the customer can signal those serving him that he wants attention (that is,
signal him to engage in direct "focused" interaction). In the ordinary
restaurant, as Goffman points out, the waiter, rushed by demands from a
number of tables, can pretend not to see the signal of a customer at a given
table and thus give himself more time to finish what he is in the process of
doing. In the expensive restaurant, where a waiter is assigned to wait on only
one party at a time, the patron is freed from the annoyance of these delays
and can expect immediate response to signals for attention.

This is more broadly a problem in the organization of "partly focused"
interaction (see p. 11). Waiters are present with the "main participants" (the
diners), but are excluded from their "focused" conversation or interaction
except when summoned to take part. The condition of summons is linked to
the relative status of those involved. The higher the relative status of the
"main participants" and the more they are paying for the service, the smaller
the cue required to signal and command immediate attention. Summoning
others to engage in "focused" interaction is typically a prerogative of status.
Those of lower status are expected to be available to such summons while not
normally initiating them themselves. Thus, in an illustration mentioned by
Goffman, the butler who wishes to engage his master does not normally
directly initiate interaction, but may "cough" discreetly to attract his notice.
For further discussion of these matters, see Goffman, *Behavior in Public
Places,* p. 91ff.

7. We refer to waiters rather than waitresses here because exclusive
restaurants typically employ males to serve and attend to their clientele. This
suggests that male attention is deemed more valuable. While attention-giving
is expected more regularly of women, the dominant classes have the resources
to purchase male attention as a scarce and more prized commodity.

focus of the interaction. This can involve considerable finesse, as in the case of the headwaiter, who is expected to speak with a certain elegance befitting an attendant of a distinguished patron, but not in a style that calls undue notice to himself.

The waiter-patron interchange in the expensive restaurant reflects the way attention is typically allocated in formal interactions, with people in the dominant classes gaining the attention and members of the subordinate classes giving it. Since attention-giving is related to offering deference and respect, the transaction not only reflects the economic power of those in the giving and getting roles, but symbolically affirms their relative social worth.[8]

The privileged classes purchase attention not only in restaurants, shops, and other public settings, but also in formal interactions in private life, by employing attention-givers in the home. As depicted in chronicles of upper-class life, such as the popular television series "Upstairs, Downstairs," members of the dominant classes have historically surrounded themselves with servants recruited from the subordinate classes who must routinely give attention to whomever pays for their services. Even in the contemporary affluent household, cooks, cleaning ladies, governesses, and other domestic help are employed in attention-giving roles and are judged partly by the quality of the attention they give.[9] In many upper-class homes, liveried servants continue to

---

8. An interesting analogy is suggested between the selling of labor power and the selling of attention. In the capitalist market system, both labor and attention are transformed into commodities, with purchase reserved for the dominant classes. The analogy is imperfect in certain ways, as members of the dominant classes, for example, therapists, doctors, lawyers, also sell their attention on the market. They market it, however, for a much higher price and command a much higher return.

9. These roles require the sustaining of the cognitive focus of attention in all role-related interaction on those who employ them. The role is thus comprised of a set of face-to-face interactions, both "focused" and "partly focused" in which the servant surrenders the focus of attention to his master or boss. Since it is not appropriate for the servant, except under special circumstances, to introduce himself or herself as the focus, he or she assumes a role-defined invisibility, discussed further on pp. 78 ff.

Richard Parker indicates that the employment of "domestic help" has declined considerably in the upper class since World War II, with only one in five households employing regular help. Nonetheless, Gabriel Kolko has pointed out that 2.5 million butlers, maids, chauffeurs, and cooks are still employed in private households, predominantly from the upper class. See serve dinner, while valets and chauffeurs attend to the adults. The privileged classes are also able to purchase "overseers" (nannies, governesses, etc.) for their children, thus relieving parents of many attention-giving responsibilities.

Wealth and Informal Interactions: Attention and Consumption Displays

Attention is "purchased" in a different way in the informal interactions of everyday life. By displaying symbols of material success, an individual can increase his sense of his own worth and his rights to attention, while at the same time predisposing others to give the attention expected. Ostentatious or subtle exhibits of property can be used both to attract attention in public places and to help a person maintain the focus of attention in everyday conversations.[10]

Displays of clothing are the most important evidences of property in ordinary interaction. Dressing fashionably is an extremely common means by which people seek to gain attention. Here, members of the dominant classes are especially advantaged, as they define style and can best afford to dress glamorously. For example:

> Two women were sitting over lunch in the restaurant
> associated with the museum. A third woman, elegantly
> coiffured and stylishly dressed, sat down to join them.
> In greeting her, her friends immediately focused their

Richard Parker, *The Myth of the Middle Class,* p. 125, and Gabriel Kolko, *Wealth and Power in America.*

10. Consumption displays bring both "focused" and "unfocused" face-to-face attention. In conversation and other focused interactions, the receptivity of others to an individual's conversational initiatives are significantly affected by his perceived worth. As indicated in the first chapter, external signs of high status play in important role by predisposing others to give credibility to one's statements, to see more humor and sophistication in one's jokes, and, more broadly, to yield the floor and give attention in deference to perceived power or authority. In "unfocused" interactions, where people are physically together in the same space but are not engaged in talk (as in the subway car or theater), property displays are effective in attracting visual attention. Under circumstances of "conspicuous consumption," as Veblen emphasizes, this is normally associated with unexpressed sentiments of respect, admiration, or envy. See Thorsten Veblen, *The Portable Veblen,* pp. 111ff.

attention on her, looking intently at her outfit and commenting on how lovely she looked. Both commented specifically about her dress and she began to talk at some length about the dress itself and her experiences in shopping for it. The other women, after a few minutes, began to try to broaden the conversation and bring in some of their own shopping experience. By returning to one or another feature of the very striking dress she was wearing, the woman who had been dominating the conversation continued to redirect the conversation to her own clothes and experiences in shopping. The others subsided into a permanent listening role, only letting their attention wander occasionally when they scrutinized the outfits of other elegantly dressed women who were walking by.

Here, a stylish woman focuses the conversation on herself by referring constantly to her clothes. Clothing has special importance for women, who are taught to seek attention through glamor and sexuality. Moreover, women in the dominant classes can use their economic resources to gain added advantages not available to less affluent women in daily interactions. While the latter also learn to rely heavily on clothing to gain attention, they cannot normally afford the expensive jewelry, elegant wardrobes and other glamorous or very stylish items that win privileged women extra attention.[11]

The automobile is another possesion that symbolizes social worth and is "displayed" to bring attention to the self. By driving such luxury cars as Cadillacs, Continentals, Mercedes, and Rolls Royces, wealthy individuals attract attention in the streets and in public places.[12] One millionaire's "outsize white Cadillac with a gold plated dashboard" has been described by C. Wright Mills as a

11. The privileges of class here are defined by standards of taste and elegance. Less privileged women, who adorn themselves with a profusion of gaudy costume jewelry, will command less attention than a privileged woman wearing simple strands of gems encased in precious metals.

12. This is the "unfocused" attention that people receive from strangers with whom they are not directly interacting. Most displays of conspicuous consumption are useful in attracting such "unfocused" attention as well as "focused" attention in conversation. See Chapter 1, pp. 11 ff.

lavish example from an earlier era. Nowadays, the acquisition of expensive but less blatantly garish vehicles, including sports cars, antique automobiles, and chauffeured limousines remain a means by which dominant groups indirectly "purchase" attention. [13]

There are many other areas in which dominant groups set standards of taste and draw attention by displays of consumer sophistication. Tasteful displays of furniture, art work, glassware, china and cutlery, stereophonic equipment, and other household items are used by members of affluent groups as subtle ways of establishing their worth and rights to special attention in everyday interactions.

In consumer economies, through advertising, members of subordinate classes also learn to depend on clothes, cars, and other consumer goods as attention-getting commodities. Advertising successfully persuades consumers that without certain products they will appear either ugly, uncultivated, or offensive, leading others to withdraw attention. Listerine ads warn people of the consequences of bad breath, cosmetic ads condemn unsightly, pimpled, or wrinkled skin. Buying commodities thus helps reduce personal anxieties about getting attention; if most members of the society cannot afford to buy the clothes and other expensive goods to make them fashionable or "glamorous" like the upper classes, at least they can avoid the "blemishes" that might mar their appearance by making relatively inexpensive consumer purchases. [14]

Subordinate groups also buy goods to attract desireable attention. A given toothpaste will buy a winning smile with sparkling white teeth; a given perfume will attract and hold the attention of that glamorous man in the office. People in the subordinate classes, without access to institutional attention-getting roles, may come to depend especially on the acquisition of goods to compensate. The worker in the factory or the clerk in the

---

13. The importance of automobiles, and a twist on class privileges, is suggested by a recent advertisement for a dependable compact. A tycoon shown at the wheel, when asked why he chooses this car when he can afford to drive any car he wants, retorts, "I can also afford not to." Those with the most unassailable status thus do not require constant commodity displays.
14. See Stewart Ewen, *Captains of Conciousness.*

office who get little or no attention in their work roles may be able to afford the flashy car, clothes, and other goods that bring some attention in personal interaction. While for many consumption is one of the few avenues for gaining attention, it is part of a system that best serves the privileged classes, as they can purchase the commodities which most symbolize worth.

We have examined some of the ways in which monied groups purchase attention in formal interactions and in everyday social life. One further point about the relation between money and attention, particularly in regard to the poor,[15] deserves discussion. We suggested earlier that the attention-getting role is normally the powerful one,[16] but there are exceptions affecting mainly the poor. A number of institutions, including welfare agencies, social work offices, and employment services, offer poor people roles in which they receive face-to-face attention. However, power in these interactions rests in the hands of those giving attention. Welfare client, as an example, is a role of weakness and helplessness, bringing attention at the cost of respect and requiring that the individual acknowledge personal incapacity, failure, or dependency.

Under these conditions, the attention-getting role is one the individual would ordinarily avoid. Those receiving such attention are less likely to feel supported or nurtured as intruded upon, violated, or humiliated. They have little control over the nature of the interaction and the attention given, or over how the parts of their personalities and life histories are examined and revealed. While attention is always potentially controlling or victimizing, this is especially true when the attention-giver represents social control agencies. Giving attention becomes part of the exercise of power and the attention itself a threat or weapon.[17]

15. As indicated earlier, the poor are a relatively small sector of the subordinate classes, and face the greatest problems of visibility in formal interactions.

16. See p. 40.

17. Studies of the interactional process in welfare offices and in public hospitals serving the poor make this abundantly clear. Frederick Wiseman's film *Welfare* is an especially powerful document in this regard. See also Erving Goffman, *Asylums.*

Attention and Work

In addition to being a commodity that can be purchased, attention is a reward of authority and prestige in work. People in the dominant occupations[18] gain special attention in the formal interactions in their work life and also in their informal interactions in personal life. This is related both to the structure of work roles and to the growing importance of work as the governing symbol of social worth.

The claim to expertise is a primary source of power for those in dominant occupations and a formidable way of gaining attention. People approach most professionals for what they believe is valuable information, and not only pay generously for it, but give in return an uncommonly close form of attention.[19] The worried patient will hang on every word of his doctor, the legal client will listen keenly to the advice of his lawyer, the avid student will give undivided attention to the professor who knows what the student wants to know. Professionals frequently use "displays" of knowledge to capture attention:

> This professor had an air of expertise that was extremely
> effective in capturing and holding the attention of his
> students. During the lecture, he referred constantly to
> the books he had written, as well as the one he was cur-
> rently writing. These references seemed to have an

18. By dominant occupations, we mean those in the professional-managerial class vested with economic, political, and cultural authority. These fall primarily under the Department of Labor's occupational titles of "proprietary" or "professional and managerial." The discussion that follows applies to some degree to the middle-level technical or administrative positions, but mainly to the prestigious professional and top managerial roles occupied primarily by white males of the privileged classes.

19. Students of professionalism have shown that the authority of professionals rests on the claim to hold exclusive specialized knowledge. The authority of managers in the workplace is also legitimated by their exclusive claim to knowledge of the production process. Nicos Poulantzas has argued that differences in knowledge—or, more accurately, claims to knowledge established by educational credentials—serve as the major cultural legitimation of class privileges. The analysis that follows explores this theme in regard to privileges of attention in face-to-face interactions. Poulantzas' general argument is developed in his *Classes in Contemporary Capitalism.*

effect, as students whose attention had been wandering refocused their gaze on him at these points.

More subtle displays are also common:

The teacher is unpretentious and one of those rare instructors who makes it clear that he is not an absolute expert in the field. He confesses this fact frequently during the class. Laughing it off, he gains power and attention by giving the tacit implication that he knows more than he would admit to. Students keep their eyes riveted on him and do not stare out the window, whisper to each other or show other signs of diverted attention.

A professional is normally granted attention automatically on the basis of assumed expertise and knowledge. A resort to concious "displays," even of the subtle kind illustrated here, is thus likely to happen only under those circumstances—which occur frequently in the classroom—where the professional is uncertain that those required by their role to listen to him are actually doing so.[20]

The control of rewards and punishments also assures professionals and managers attention in formal interactions. In a courtroom, all parties extend respectful attention to the judge, not only because of the ritual formalities but because of the inordinate power he wields over the fate of the petitioners.[21] Similarly, at the

---

20. It should be noted that teachers are given direct formal control over the allocation of attention in the classroom. This is institutionalized in the mechanism of hand-raising, which allows the teacher to determine who is the focus of attention at any given moment. In most work settings, those in authority are given the formal power of the chairman over attention in office meetings and other structured interactions at the workplace.

21. The attention-dynamics of the courtroom were highlighted in an unusual fashion during the Vietnam war period in the farcical trial of the "Chicago Seven," when the antiwar defendants refused to abide by normal courtroom ritual and to extend the appropriate respect to Judge Julius Hoffman. Using theatrical techniques, on the one hand, they drew disproportionate attention to themselves and their own political ideas, while also successfully exploiting Hoffman's formally structured "center stage" position and manipulating his visibility to create a notorious symbol of Establishment bigotry and ineptness.

workplace, because the employer hires and fires, and controls conditions of work, employees focus on him. In face-to-face interactions with her boss, a subordinate must give respectful attention even if she feels resentment or bitterness. This is a part of deference in formal interactions: the role of the subordinate is not only to listen and respond to instructions or commands, but also to show respect by being especially attentive and taking care not to draw undue attention to herself.[22]

Professional services have traditionally required attention-giving to clients in face-to-face interactions.[23] More recently, however, changes in professional work roles have shifted attention-giving responsibility from professionals to less skilled subordinates; the professional spends less of his time in interactions with clients and, during the time he does so, often gains attention as the "expert" rather than giving it as a helper. These changes are well illustrated in the following observation in a private hospital room:

> The patient is resting in a single room two days after abdominal surgery. She is seen primarily by nurses and aides who enter the room every couple of hours to check vital signs and the I.V. The major attending nurse is solicitous and personally attentive. In the early afternoon she enters and asks how the patient is feeling. The patient smiles and indicates she is feeling stronger. She then says she is feeling more pain around the incision. She describes the pain and the nurse listens attentively. The nurse sits on the bed and feels carefully around the abdominal area. She touches her gently and with some nurturance. She tells the patient there is no indication of infection or other problems, but she should let her know about any acute pain that develops. She is reassuring and supportive. She also in-

22. This aspect of deference has been explored by Erving Goffman in a number of pioneering essays. See especially "The Nature of Deference and Demeanor" in Goffman, *Interaction Ritual* and *Behavior in Public Places,* pp. 90ff.

23. Few work roles are purely attention-getting or attention-giving, but are a blend of the two, with a greater emphasis on one posture or the other. While the dominant occupational roles have elements of attention-giving, these are being reduced in ways elaborated below.

dicates that the doctor, whom the patient has seen only once since the operation, will be coming to see her in the afternoon.

The doctor arrives an hour later. He is friendly, but formal and personally remote. He asks how the patient is doing; as she answers, he does not look at her but at a chart he is holding. He asks her a few questions in quick succession, now looking at the patient, but indicating by his manner that he does not have much time. She then asks quickly about her abdominal condition. She is interested in the exact prognosis of the disorder. He then begins a rather lengthy, authoritative description of the disease. He seems to enjoy talking about it and expounds on it for about five minutes. The attention in the interaction remains clearly focused on him for the rest of the time, and he leaves right after his exposition.

The difference in the two interactions is striking. With the nurse, the focus of attention remains on the patient and the nurse exhibits a "bedside manner" traditionally associated with family doctors. The doctor, on the other hand, interacts with the patient less as a caretaker than as expert consultant. In the "expert" role he becomes the focus of attention himself and offers relatively little attention to the patient.

The same dynamics are evident in higher education. Professors are "experts" who meet with students in large classes to impart knowledge. To the extent that students receive any attention, they are less likely to receive it from their professors in the classroom than from teaching assistants or graduate students who lead discussion groups, read papers, and meet with students in individual consultations. Like nurses and medical paraprofessionals, teaching assistants are part of an emerging stratum of subordinates who buffer professionals from demands of clients and take over the routine burden of attention-giving.

In the business world executives and bosses also delegate much of the responsibility of attention-giving to subordinates. The secretary-receptionist, for example, not only gives attention to clients, but must do so in a way conducive to her boss's interests. Secretaries give attention to their bosses as well as to clients, nurses to doctors as well as patients, and teaching assistants to professors as well as to students. These attention-givers thus benefit those in dominant occupations doubly, not only by lightening their attention-giving responsibilities but reinforcing their attention-getting status.[24]

Invisibility at Work: Subordinate Occupations

The work roles of those not in dominant occupations are rarely attention-getting ones. Most sales and service workers, clerical workers, and industrial workers do not have subordinates expected to give them attention. The only attention that these workers can typically expect in their formal interactions is from supervisors who regulate their behavior.[25]

It is useful to distinguish subordinate workers who remain visible and others who become invisible. Invisibility, as R. D. Laing has pointed out, is the most drastic form of attention-deprivation, ultimately more painful and dehumanizing than hostile or other "negative" attention. Anyone can become temporarily invisible in meetings, groups, and other kinds of everyday situations. But for those whose job is regarded as dirty, unpleasant, or unsightly, and

---

24. In this way, secretaries and other subordinate attention-givers in the work world play an analogous role to dominant groups as domestic servants who, as we have already seen, are hired as attention-givers in the private sphere. In her analysis of the role of the secretary, Mary Benet indicates that her duties approximate those of a wife and servant combined: "She makes his plane reservations, protects him from subordinates, does his expense accounts, sends Christmas cards and listens to his domestic problems." Benet goes on to indicate that in face-to-face interactions with the boss, the secretary takes on a certain kind of invisibility and cannot expect any attention except a flirtatious or sexual kind that she may not desire. The delegation of the attention-giving role thus follows sex-role prescriptions, as secretaries, nurses, and receptionists are typically female while their bosses are characteristically male. See Mary Benet, *The Secretarial Ghetto*, pp. 72ff.

25. In informal interactions, as Robert Schrank has recently stressed, workers do give and get face-to-face attention from other workers in the "schmoozing" or sociability that is one of the most important and gratifying aspects of work life. Schrank shows, however, that the right to socialize is enjoyed most fully by professionals and others in dominant occupations, as rules, regimentation, and the noise of machines restrict informal interactions among most industrial and clerical workers. See Robert Schrank, *Ten Thousand Working Days.*

are therefore required to work in hidden places such as kitchens or basements, it is routine to their daily experience. Other workers of very low status, such as the cleaning lady or the busboy, while they may work in the purview of other people, remain invisible because others feel no need to acknowledge their presence.[26]

Erving Goffman's distinction between "front" and "back" regions of the workplace provides a basis for looking more closely at the difference between visible and invisible work roles. Goffman points out that work space can be divided into that accessible to the public or other outsiders (the "front" space) and those accessible only to the employees themselves (the "back" region). In a restaurant, the kitchen and stockroom are the back regions, while the diningroom is the front region. There are normally physical barriers between front and back regions, designed to prevent those in the front regions from seeing what takes place in the back regions. Certain workers, such as waitresses, have access to both regions while others, such as dishwashers, are confined to the back region.

Goffman was primarily concerned with understanding work as a kind of performance, and considered the back region as a backstage where the actors prepare the props and mobilize themselves for the drama in the front region. For our purposes, the distinction between front and back regions is useful in understanding who gives and gets attention. Those restricted to the front region can never give or get attention from those restricted to the back region and vice-versa.

Workers restricted to the back regions become invisible to the public. The kitchen help, for example, remain completely unseen by the clientele of the restaurant. Similarly, stockboys, packers,

---

26. In the first chapter we defined invisibility as the position of the person in ordinary conversation or any other "focused" face-to-face interaction who receives no attention from others in the interaction. The notion of invisibility is extended here to refer also to those who suffer role-defined exclusion from others with whom they are physically proximate but are not engaged in "focused" face-to-face interaction. This includes workers in "partly focused" interactions who have official status as participants in the situation but are excluded from the conversation or gaze of the others involved. Many of the examples of invisible workers that follow, including the discussion of kitchen help, janitors, and domestics, refer to invisibility in "partly focused" settings and interactions rather than the fully "focused" interactions discussed earlier.

inventory clerks, and many clerical workers, who are normally restricted to back regions of department stores, grocery stores, and other service or retail establishments, also work unnoticed.

Being in an invisible work role does not imply that the worker gets no attention at all in his job. The dishwasher may seek and get attention in informal interactions with fellow workers in his back region. Moreover, he is freed from having to give attention to the clientele. Nonetheless, his invisibility to the public is symbolic of his low worth and disadvantages him in gaining attention.[27] Symbolically, it suggests that he is not entitled to acknowledgement or recognition from the clientele.

Workers confined to the back regions are not the only ones in invisible work roles. A more extreme form of dehumanization is experienced by those who work in front regions, but whose presence commands no attention whatsoever. The sweeper in the restaurant, for example, carries out his work in full view without anyone else noticing him and remains unseen unless he commits an offense which violates his role. In the movie *Charlie,* for example, the hero, a busboy, is portrayed in his invisible role until he drops and breaks a stack of dishes, thus exploding out of his invisible position. Similarly, transportation workers, and the janitors and groundskeepers in many establishments carry out their work in view of others and yet receive minimal recognition. A cleaning lady or other domestic servants may glide through the house performing her duties almost as a ghost, without family members taking any note of her presence.[28]

On the other hand, there are many work settings where the lower-status employees occupy the front regions while those with

27. Invisibility from the public is a special form of invisibility in "partly focused" settings. It is unique because it involves clear physical separation from others to whom one's services are directed. Other workers, such as busboys, who enter the front region but are not acknowledged, suffer a different kind. They can be physically seen by the public, but are systematically ignored. This second form is discussed further in the paragraph that follows.

28. This form of invisibility is characteristic of all "partly focused" interactions where people such as waiters and cleaners are expected to be physically present but are excluded from the "focused" interaction of the main participants. Since it is only workers of very low status who are assigned the "invisible" position in such settings, this suggests that their invisibility is a symbolic representation of their degraded moral status.

the greatest power are sheltered in exclusive back regions. In a bank, for example, the tellers are visible, while the executives are hidden within imposing offices. Similarly, in many bureaucracies, clerks and other low-status office workers can normally be seen within a large office space while the more powerful employees gradually disappear into asylums as they move up the ranks. In these circumstances, "invisibility" is actually a symbol of status. The executive suite is, however, a very different kind of back region from, say, the restaurant kitchen, and the "invisibility" of the high official radically distinct from that of the dishwasher. The executive office is designed to serve the interest of the one who occupies it, functioning in many ways as a sanctuary from the demands of others. Moreover, the executive is invisible only when he chooses, as he has a staff of subordinate attention-givers (secretaries, personal aides, etc.) on whom he can call at any time. He also has access to the front region and can demand, if he desires, a great deal of attention from subordinates when he enters there.

Workers available to the public, moreover, such as bank tellers and receptionists, are normally in attention-giving roles. They typically receive from the public only the minimal acknowledgment of their presence that is required to conduct business. Their visibility merely reflects the obligation of giving attention to customers—a duty delegated to those in the front region—and not the privilege of receiving it, which is reserved for those in the back region.

As indicated earlier, all lower-status workers are assured, however, of getting the one kind of attention that all work establishments direct toward their employees, even the least favored in formal interactions: supervisory attention.[29] Employers extend the attention required to insure that they are doing their job, maintaining discipline, and working at the rhythm and efficiency

---

29. Supervisory attention occurs in both "focused" and "partly focused" settings. The worker becomes the focus of supervisory attention in "focused" interactions when the supervisor engages in direct face-to-face talk with him, as when he verbally instructs him or admonishes him. More often, supervisory attention is given in "partly focused" situations, where the supervisor is watching the workers and monitoring their behavior but is not conversing with them or otherwise engaging in "focused" interaction.

expected of them. On the assembly line, the foreman focuses his attention on the workers to regulate their behavior and prevent interruptions of the production process. The gaze of the foreman is the immediate expression, face-to-face, of a larger system of social control that institutionalizes the power of the employer over the worker; it is the most important and least desired of the forms of attention that workers receive.

Work Identity and Informal Interaction

We have seen that the competition for attention in ordinary informal interaction involves a struggle by each individual to establish his or her relative worth. High occupational status has become one of the most important symbols defining personal worth in ordinary social relations. As a result, professionals, executives, and others in dominant occupations enjoy a significant advantage in seeking and winning attention in ordinary conversation.

The importance of occupational status derives from the primacy of "ability" as a contemporary measure of worth. Richard Sennett has shown that ability (and accomplishment) has become a universal value that significantly affects the appraisal of members of all classes of their own worth and that of others. Occupational status is considered in modern culture the most tangible and compelling measure of ability and now carries the symbolic significance that wealth had in an earlier period.[30]

To exploit occupational status as a means of getting attention, the individual must successfully display or communicate it to others. Obviously, a doctor cannot expect special attention in conversation unless he has made his professional identity known. Unlike a property display, disclosures of occupational identity are

---

30. This reflects the prevailing view of the social order, and the occupational structure specifically, as meritocratic. In a meritocracy, the place on the occupational ladder achieved by each person is understood as a reflection of his own abilities. This perception of the social structure is consistent with the ideology of individualism in contemporary culture and serves to legitimate the class system itself. For a discussion of these issues, see Richard Sennett and Jonathan Cobb, *The Hidden Injuries of Class.*

not usually communicated visually (although a doctor, for example, can give visual cues by wearing a "beeper" or his white coat when off the job). Such information normally surfaces in conversation either by being openly discussed or by being subtly communicated through use of technical language or knowledge. A doctor's professional identity will normally become apparent to strangers or acquaintances when he talks directly about his work, uses some kind of medical vocabulary, or steers the discussion to health-related topics in which he has expertise. At the beginning of conversations between strangers or new acquaintances, people normally break the ice with the familiar question "What do you do?" Occupation is thus revealed at the outset and helps to establish the relative status of the parties talking and the allocation of attention.

In most social relations, those in dominant occupations need not disclose this information, as it is already known to family, friends, and others with whom they regularly interact. As such, their occupational status is a permanently recognized "badge of ability" that establishes their special worth in the eyes of others and, in most informal situations, enhances their perceived rights to attention. As indicated earlier fathers in high status jobs often gain added attention in their families because of the prestige they carry from the outside world. Those who cannot exhibit the occupational "badge" or whose occupational status is clearly inferior, will find their worth constantly in question. In order to win attention, they must struggle to establish it in other ways. This is reflected in subtle dynamics in conversations among people of different occupational statuses. People of low status may feel the pressure to talk constantly simply to prevent others from withdrawing their attention altogether. This is reflected in the stereotypical "talkativeness" of housewives, who cannot draw on occupational status to secure attention in ordinary situations. An analysis of the talk of working-class housewives indicates that their lack of occupational status forces them to seek alternative strategies (obsessive talking is one possibility) to mitigate the fear that they might be completely disregarded.[31]

---

31. See Peter Trudgill, "Sex, Covert Prestige and Linguistic Change in the Urban British English of Norwich," in Thorne and Henley (eds.), *Language and Society,* pp. 88-104.

Attention and Education

An individual's education also has a major effect on the attention he receives in everyday interactions. Since access to higher education depends on one's class position[32] and is instrumental in one's gaining entry to dominant occupations, it becomes an indirect basis for access to the attention-getting roles already considered. In addition, independently of one's occupation and income, one's education can be a powerful claim on attention. In everyday conversation, people with college or advanced education have a number of advantages in gaining attention, stemming from the importance of schooling as a unique symbol of worth that entitles the individual to special forms of recognition.

This is partly due to the widespread tendency to equate schooling with intelligence. Intelligence is regarded as a fundamental kind of ability which commands enormous respect in contemporary culture, and its appearance or apparent absence has a major effect on the kinds of attention any individual receives. While there is no compelling evidence that those given special access to higher education are more intelligent than others, they are normally regarded as such, in part because education provides resources (mainly verbal skills and specialized information) for appearing so. Those without advanced education are widely considered deficient both in ability and intelligence, and thus lacking a claim to the interest and attention of others.

Education is also a badge or symbol of "self-development," another contemporary measure of worth, related to ability, but more explicitly concerned with the extent to which talents, skills, and faculties have been cultivated and actualized (in a sense, the extent to which ability has been realized). The criterion of self-development means that those perceived as most "evolved" or "accomplished" are viewed as especially deserving of attention.[33]

---

32. Members of dominant classes have the greatest resources to pursue higher education and are most likely to do so. Extensive research in the United States has demonstrated this empirical relation between education and class. See especially Jerome Karabel, "Community Colleges and Social Stratification," *Harvard Educational Review*.

33. The ethos of self-development, while conceived by educators such as John Dewey or psychologists such as Carl Rogers as an expression of humanistic culture, thus becomes, in a highly individualistic and competitive society, a

Revelations about educational status are enormously important in shaping others' assessments of one's worth and regulating the flow of attention. People in dominant classes rely on their education as a major sign both of their "self-development" and their special rights to attention. Whenever the rights are in doubt, educated individuals will normally act to reaffirm their worth, often by displaying some expression of self development or schooling. This display can be compared to the property or consumer display described earlier, by which individuals exhibit evidence of wealth. One does not ordinarily make explicit reference to educational accomplishments, although an individual who offhandedly mentions his undergraduate experience at Princeton or the fact that he has a Ph.D. will enhance his status. Usually, the display is more subtle and indirect, involving either the use of sophisticated vocabulary and manner of speaking or the display of specialized knowledge.

Speech is enormously important as an education display and attention-getting cue. Sociolinguists have accumulated considerable evidence that people can be identified in terms of class, subculture, and education on the basis of how they talk.[34] Such matters as vocabulary, grammar, intonation, and diction significantly affect how people respond to one another. Members of dominant classes use an expanded vocabulary (including more technical, literary, or simply "big" words) as well as the "proper" or "standard" grammar and diction that others recognize as evidence of advanced schooling. Members of subordinate classes are likely to find themselves at a disadvantage when seeking attention in any face-to-face setting in which people of different classes are brought together. On the basis of speech patterns and other cues of educational background and class position, their ideas are less likely to be taken seriously, and others less disposed to cede air time or listen attentively to them. Studies in such

means of differentiating and stratifying people. It serves as the basis for a new hierarchy, a form of psychological meritocracy, in which attention and other psychological rewards are allocated to those on top.

34. See William Labov, *Sociolinguistic Patterns; The Social Stratification of English in New York City* (Washington D.C.: Center for Applied Linguistics, 1966); Roger W. Shuy, Walter A. Wolfram, and William K. Riley, *Linguistic Correlates of Social Stratification in Detroit Speech.*

diverse contexts as jury rooms, parent-teacher meetings, and community gatherings indicate that those who talk the most frequently and whose ideas are given the greatest attention are invariably individuals with high educational status and class background, and that those less educated normally speak less often and receive less attention.[35]

Members of subordinate classes who do not exhibit the "standard" vocabulary, grammar, and diction are handicapped as soon as they begin to speak. These handicaps begin early in life, since the working- or lower-class child is less likely to get attention from teachers in school because of the way he talks.[36] This experience is reproduced in adult life in most organizations and institutions; bureaucrats, employers, and others in positions of authority, attuned to the class symbols of worth, are likely to direct attention preferentially on the basis of speech cues indicating education and class status. This is one of the most subtle forms of discrimination by class, reproduced in the everyday interactions within all our institutions.

---

35. See studies summarized in A. Paul Hare (ed.) *Handbook of Small Group Research* pp. 212ff.
36. See, for example, P.W. Jackson *Life in Classrooms,* and Robert Rosenthal and Lenore Jacobson, *Pygmalion in the Classroom.*

Chapter 5

On One's Own: *The Overburdened Self and the Need for Attention*

We know well enough that the isolation of the individual—a narrow minded egotism—is everywhere the fundamental principle of modern society. . . . The disintegration of society into individuals each guided by his private principles and each pursuing his own aims, has been pushed to its furthest limits. . . .

FREDERICK ENGELS, from *The Condition of the Working-Class in England*

The compulsive preoccupation with being seen, or simply with being visible, suggests that we must be dealing with underlying fantasies of not being seen, of being invisible.

R.D. LAING, from *The Divided Self*

Paradise is gone for good; the individual stands alone and faces the world . . .

ERICH FROMM, from *Escape From Freedom*

I have described dehumanizing patterns of interaction and attention-behavior. To consider how change in these patterns might occur, several essential questions must be asked. To what degree can the allocation of attention be cooperative and mutually supportive rather than competitive? To what extent can a psychology oriented toward giving attention be realized? Can inequalities in the distribution of attention be altered and definitions of social worth changed so that no group is regarded as unworthy of attention?

For such changes in everyday behavior to occur, the larger society itself must be transformed. Attention-dynamics are shaped by cultural values, character structure, and the distribution of power. I have emphasized that the allocation of attention inevitably mirrors the basic structure of the society in which it evolves; it can thus assume a new form only if fundamental social change occurs.

The two central patterns in America—the competitive seeking of attention and the allocation of attention to socially dominant groups—subtly reflect the prevailing individualism and class structure. We have seen that competitiveness for attention mirrors broader forms of competition, just as inequalities of attention follow wider social inequalities. It is these roots in the larger society that need more explicit consideration.

I have discussed how attention-behavior in informal social life bears a strong resemblence to behavior in the marketplace: that is, each individual takes initiative on his own behalf with only minimum concern for the well-being of others. Such individualism is rooted in cultural norms extending far beyond attention-behavior. In the economic arena, individual initiative and responsibility for oneself are fundamental imperatives. Where norms of self-interest govern economic behavior, face-to-face social behavior is also invariably egoistic and competitive. While cultures are never totally integrated, a society cannot—without great tension—create demands of competitive behavior in the economic sphere and cooperative behavior in social life. The internalization of economic rules of self-interest breeds a psychological readiness to act egoistically even in the most intimate arenas of personal life. Such economic conditioning of psychological activity has been recognized by many theorists, most notably Erich Fromm, who has used such notions as the "marketing personality" to illustrate the influence of the capitalist system on psychology and personal relations.[1]

The self-orientation that pervades American social character is rooted in a "social" individualism that grows out of economic individualism: each person functions as an independent, isolated "self," whose survival and success depend on his own resources.

---

1. See Erich Fromm, *The Sane Society.*

With few exceptions, all people exist apart from any encompassing community upon which their fortunes depend. Since the individual is thrown onto his own resources, he must of necessity be primarily focused on himself and on satisfying his own needs.[2] Let us look more closely, then, at the ways in which such social atomization (or "disaffiliation") render the individual less willing and capable of giving attention and more needy and desirous of taking it.

Self-Orientation and "Social" Individualism:
The Individual on His Own

Insecurity underlies the attention-psychology of the self-oriented individual, an insecurity rooted in aloneness, the necessity of achieving self-sufficiency economically and socially, and the imperative of demonstrating uniqueness and special merit as an individual. As Fromm has suggested, people in an individualistic society experience feelings ranging from vague apprehension to acute panic about their economic and social isolation and their capacity to cope without community support. This insecurity intensifies preoccupation with oneself and has a major bearing on face-to-face behavior. It heightens one's own needs for attention and reduces the ability to give it, as one becomes riveted on one's own needs and fears.

Aloneness heightens the need for attention simply as a consequence of social deprivation. Notwithstanding the cultural ethos of "togetherness," individualistic society has increasingly transformed everyday life into isolated, privatized pursuits in which individuals learn to act and spend time alone. This is reflected in the increasing number of single people and in the new pervasive-

---

2. As Fromm and others have stressed, this thrusting of the individual "on his own" is at the very heart of social individualism. The individual necessarily feels more vulnerable under these conditions and less protected from danger than in community-centered societies, where he is protected by the group from perils of the environment. As Lasch has recently pointed out, this sense of endangerment is closely associated with the development of self-orientation, and is closely related to the narcissism emerging in the contemporary American character. See Erich Fromm, *Escape From Freedom,* and Christopher Lasch, *The Culture of Narcissism.*

ness of privatized leisure pursuits, such as watching television, over such social activities as games or simple conversation. Because they are engaged in fewer activities with others, many people develop intensified needs for attention. An extreme example is the elderly, left alone for long periods. The self-oriented character, when entering the company of others, typically craves attention and redirects it to himself.

Yet it is not simply lack of social contact but the burdens of coping on one's own that contribute most powerfully to insecurity and yearning for attention. Since the individual lacks enduring group or community support, he attempts to transform each individual encounter into a support vehicle that can compensate for his underlying vulnerability. He is impelled to seek attention to alleviate exacerbated daily stresses and difficulties—an approach that must fail not only because interactions with other dis-affiliated persons can never provide the community support he seeks, but also because each self-oriented person seeks the attention the other requires.

Yet another factor is the precarious sense of worth experienced in individualistic societies. Each person's basic value is conditional upon his demonstrating his uniqueness and particular merit. The cultural pressures to prove one's distinctive individuality, and thus to claim one's moral rights as a full person, leads Americans to labor under the apprehension that they may not be regarded as worthy or acceptable by others, and induces a profound in-security.[3] Under individualism, the person becomes self-oriented, then, because his value is so deeply in question. The culture perpetually redirects him to a focus on his own individuality, while simultaneously heightening his insecurity regarding his merit and worth as a developed being. The self inevitably becomes an object of concern and preoccupation, a form of "negative egoism" that typifies self-oriented characters in America.

This conditionality of worth places people in continuing doubt about their own rights to attention. This anxiety may include the fear that one is not sufficiently interesting to merit attention, a feeling that reflects the need to demonstrate excite-

---

3. For a development of this thesis, see Richard Sennett and Jonathan Cobb, *The Hidden Injuries of Class.*

ment and uniqueness. While with women this uneasiness is displayed as apprehension about taking attention, it leads also to persistent efforts to gain recognition. The more one doubts one's worth or magnetism, the more important it becomes to claim attention and thereby set one's fears to rest. The self-oriented person thus persistently seeks attention, yet can never completely alleviate his doubts that he is entitled to it.

Self-Orientation and Economic Individualism

In America, economic forces and burdens lie at the heart of self-orientation. People are cut adrift from any community providing economic security. Thrown into a labor market that rewards individual performance while making employment precarious and highly competitive, each individual must become self-oriented simply to subsist and succeed.

Industrialization and capitalism imposed this economic individualism as earlier forms of community life were left shattered by the growth of the marketplace and private property and capital. Capitalism removed the control over economic life from the community, thus precipitating the decline of collectivity and the rise of the disaffiliated "self." [4]   Simultaneously, it implanted

---

4. Marx regarded the destruction of community life as an essential concomitant of the expansion of the market place and the growth of private capital. The transfer of ownership and control of economic resources, including land and capital, to capitalist forces outside the traditional community undermined its integrity. Since the communities of medieval society were based on precapitalist forms of domination and oppression, Marx did not mourn their passing. Nonetheless, in his discussion of the capitalist market's brutal reduction of human relations to self-interested calculation and naked self-interest, Marx forecast the weakening of social bonds and the ensuing rise of the disaffiliated "self."

The Marxist analysis implies an erosion of community in two stages. The first involves the destruction of feudal communities by the rise of competitive capitalism, discussed in the text. The second is the eclipse of the vestiges of community in the small town settings of competitive capitalism by the metropolitization associated with the rise of monopoly capital. Monopolization intensified processes set in motion by the competitive stage, as it removed economic control to mass corporate institutions even further removed from the community and increasingly beyond its control.

Other social theorists, many not within the Marxist tradition, have also within the individual both real and imagined individualistic notions that one's economic destiny was to be determined by one's own efforts.

Once communal beings were thus transformed into atomized agents on the labor market. As Fromm and others have stressed, tradition had previously bound the individual tightly to the community, closely regulating his economic behavior and responsibilities; while restricted in his freedom and mobility, each person had a security, assured by community support and cooperation. In the new capitalist labor market, the individual was on his own. His fate was determined by his own success in selling his skills or wares. Since his relations with others were now competitive rather than cooperative, he could no longer expect group support; the burdens of survival were now his alone.

Such economic individualism bred a new focus on self. Bearing sole responsibility for one's economic fate places a fundamental strain on psychic life, resulting in intensified concern with oneself and one's own fortunes. This is another form of "negative egoism," to be interpreted not as self-celebration but a response to acute insecurity. With his attention focused on economic preoccupations and anxieties, the individual has limited ability to give attention to others in everyday interactions; his resources overtaxed, he seeks attention without capacity for reciprocation.

The capitalist marketplace, while transforming survival from a collective to an individual preoccupation, simultaneously institutionalized mobility and the dream of self-aggrandizement. In economic life, mobility induces self-orientation, for it requires sustained attention to one's own advancement. The "mobile" self is the most disaffiliated, as mobility necessarily loosens the individual's ties to community. Dreams of advancement indeed

---

analyzed the demise of community as a consequence of the displacement of economic and other functions to mass institutions, especially the corporation and the state. In his discussions of the social bases of community, Robert Nisbet has forcefully demonstrated that traditional communities survive only by carrying out social, economic, and political functions creating interdependence and meaning among their members. Nisbet emphasizes that a defining characteristic of modern society is the removal of such functions from the community-level institutions of family, neighborhood, and church to corporations and especially the state. See Robert Nisbet, *The Quest For Community* and Karl Marx and Friedrich Engels, *The German Ideology*.

presuppose a consciousness of a separate "selfhood" not highly developed in earlier eras. The mobility institutionalized by the marketplace slowly transforms the meaning of social identity itself from a secure and traditionally defined status in community to the personally defined and achieved "self."

Self-orientation becomes the consciousness of those most mobile and therefore least integrated in the community. Economically, it is expressed through such institutions as the "career," which are ways of organizing motivation and attention around the aims of the self. Particularly in the dominant classes, where prospects for mobility are strongest, careerism and visions of economic and social aggrandizement become the basis of an intensified self-absorption, while in subordinate classes, where vestiges of community (such as neighborhood and church) are stronger, self-orientation is less developed.

Within the dominant classes, economic self-orientation is readily visible in the attention-dynamics of everyday interaction. Among the most career oriented, topics of conversation revert invariably to one's work, achievements, and difficulties. Conversational narcissism takes the form of establishing whose career circumstance is more deserving of attention. Underlying these dynamics is a profound need to gain attention and support for a "self" excessively vulnerable because of its dissaffiliation and lack of community support.

Prospects for Change: Some Speculations on the Future of Individualism

The prospects for the erosion of self-orientation and egoistic attention-behavior are linked to reducing individualism. America is developing, however, not toward greater community or co-operation, but toward an intensification of the entrenched individualism. The continuing decline of the family, the neighborhood, and other "community" institutions along with the strengthening of capitalist values and institutions suggests the yet further ensnarement of the individual in the conditions originally creating his self-orientation: he is now no less responsible for his own economic fate but increasingly cut adrift from any permanent group that can support him socially. One would anticipate, then, a heightening of self-orientation and the even greater diffusion of the dehumanizing patterns of social interaction that we have described.

The deepening individualism and the potent self-orientation it evokes can be seen in contemporary cultural ideologies of "self-development" and "self-actualization." Under conditions of extreme individualism, the self becomes not simply a major but a primary focus of interest, and an ideology of self-cultivation takes root in large sectors of the population (normally the most individualized). This is associated, as Philip Reiff has brilliantly shown, both with the decline of any loyalty or attachment to community and the rise of a privatized "therapeutic" culture. Each individual is preoccupied with his own "personal growth" and increasingly incapable of transcending a highly complex but intensified egocentricity.[5]

While those within such a culture are oriented toward "personal relationships" requiring some giving of attention, the overriding commitment to oneself perpetuates the individualistic attention-dynamics. The therapeutic culture only exacerbates, in fact, the egoistic tendencies built into society, as it legitimates, on the basis of a sophisticated psychological ideology of self-actualization, the absorption of one's attention on oneself.

The growth of more humane face-to-face behavior is thus dependent on changes in society contrary to existing trends and improbable in the short run. Spiraling individualism and the intensification of self-orientation may continue, however, only until the effects of excessive individualization (and egoism) rebounds so strongly against social community and the individual herself that counteracting tendencies emerge. As Philip Slater has suggested, changes in the key features of the culture, such as its individualism, cannot be simply legislated (despite the enormous importance of changes in the economic system that can facilitate

---

5. In such a culture, the individualistic need to prove one's worth and distinctiveness as an individual is even more evident: it is a culture entirely devoted to the development of individuality. Yet the criterion of individual merit is no longer economic success but the unfolding of the most "creative" and "subtle" facets of the self. See Philip Reiff, *The Triumph of the Theraputic.*

it), but metamorphoses nonetheless can occur in response to crises generated in the society and culture. Crises in the economy, in the breakdown of social and community life, and in the mental health of individuals, all reflecting excessive individualism,[6] are likely to lead in the long run to a strengthening of latent economic, social, and psychological impulses toward collectivity and a diminishing of individualism.

The problem of how attention can be more equitably distributed is a distinct question, requiring consideration of the distribution of power and relative social worth. We have seen that allocating attention raises questions not unlike distributing wealth. There is, indeed, a close relation between the distributions of attention and wealth, as both are distributed highly unequally and those privileged in the economic sphere have many advantages in claiming more attention for themselves in daily life. Changes in the amount of attention that different groups receive is dependent on the achievement of greater equality in the larger society.

Ultimately, a humane distribution of attention can develop only in an egalitarian society, in which no group is defined as intrinsically more worthy than any other. While sexual and class inequalities persist, it is possible to identify certain changes that have already begun in America and may contribute to a more humane allocation of attention between men and women and among economic actors.

Changing Sex Roles

Men have traditionally dominated attention because of their monopolization of economic, social, and cultural power. We have seen that males gain attention by virtue of a patriarchal division of roles that assigns the major attention-giving ones to women. In

---

6. In regard to mental health, the pernicious meaning of excessive individualism was first pointed out by Emile Durkheim. In his famous study of suicide, Durkheim showed that people who live under social conditions of extreme individualism (isolation, lack of community) are particularly prone to a form of suicide he calls egoistic, one in which the individual has become so obsessively preoccupied with himself that it leads to a total rupture of consciousness with the world.

addition, patriarchy creates models of masculine and feminine personality that encourage self-orientation among men and other-orientation among women.

Changes thus depend on the redefinition of male and female roles and identity. The social definition of the female around her biological reproductive roles is the institutional basis for both the other-orientation of women and the self-orientation of men. The development of self-orientation is always linked to a structural responsibility for independent functioning in the economy and society at large—the traditional domain of the male—while other-orientation is tied to familial and child-care roles. The prolonged dependency of children, as well as the needs of infants for continuing special attention, necessitates on the part of the caretaker a transcendence of the egoistic mode; the needs of children are one of the major species considerations which power-fully counteract narcissistic tendencies and create in every society the need for some measure of other-orientation. Since child-care roles are defined in patriarchy as female, this creates constraints only against female narcissism and permits the self-orientation of the male to remain relatively unfettered.

In advanced industrial societies it is the narcissism of the male that has been acutely heightened and most urgently requires the counteracting restraint implicit in child-care roles. The intensive self-orientation of the male can change only if he is socialized to new roles that explicitly demand attentiveness to others. Since male worth is now contingent upon success in economic roles which require extraordinary self-orientation, male egoism is likely to be mitigated only by new expectations for men that involve a decline in pressures for self-directed achievement and a new emphasis on the ability to respond to people. A radical re-structuring of the primary attention-giving (i.e., child-care) roles, where men, like women, are expected to develop a capacity to give attention to children, may be the most important element in such a change.

The current trend in America is one in which women are being slowly granted access to the public sphere without major change in the roles played by men in relation to children and the home. The impact of this change on the other-orientation of women is unclear, but no fundamental transformation in male self-orientation is implied. The change in sex roles may indeed be taking a form which only reinforces the general trend in society toward greater self-orientation, that is, one which legitimates for the female the same narcissistic behavior (including attention-getting psychology) as the male, and encourages in neither sex other-orientation or the capacity to give attention. No change in sex roles, in fact, can significantly alter the egoistic, competitive organization of attention as long as economic and social conditions demand self-orientation on the part of one or both sexes. Changes broader than sex-role change are thus required.

Social Class and Social Change

The domination of attention by privileged economic groups is inevitable as long as the class structure itself persists. The essential social-psychological meaning of a class system is that one group is defined as "better" than another and thus more entitled to attention. Members of subordinate classes are always placed in a state of uncertainty about their own worth; this undercuts their capacity to assert themselves and claim greater attention.

It is appropriate to conclude with some assessment of the meaning of change in the economic system, not only because it is the only way in which the class-based inequalities can be reduced, but also because the economic system is such an important factor contributing to individualism. The economic imperative of self-interested behavior and the reigning institutions of private property and profit all enhance and intensify the individual's focus on himself. In social orders where economic institutions encourage cooperative rather than egoistic and competitive behavior, an economic basis for other-orientation is established; thus, the experience of some socialist countries suggests that transformation in the economic system limits the development of excessive individualism in the society at large and introduces strong constraints on the intensified self-orientation that plagues most Western societies.

We have seen that individualism is deeply rooted in American culture; even major changes in the economic order are not likely to completely erode the individualism entrenched in the American cultural tradition. Under conditions of greater economic security and reduced economic competition, however, individualism in American society may diminish, permitting greater concern with others. People might remain individualistic in many respects, yet become less egoistic and more capable of giving attention. This suggests at least the possibility of a less narcissistic social character and more humane social relations in which people share attention and become responsive to each other's needs.

Bibliography

Addeo, E.G., and R. Burger. *Ego Speak.* New York: Bantam, 1973.

Allen, Lucy. *Table Service.* Boston: Little Brown, 1923.

Amory, Cleveland. *The Proper Bostonians.* New York: Dutton, 1948.

Argyle, Michael, Mansur Lallee, and Mark Cook, "The Effects of Visibility on Interaction in the Dyad." *Human Relations,* 21(1968). 3-17.

Bales, Robert F. *Personality and Social Interaction.* New York: Holt, Rinehart, 1971.

———, and Talcott Parsons. *Family Socialization, and Interaction Process.* Glencoe: Free Press, 1955.

———, and Philip Slater. "Role Differentiation in Small Decision-making Groups." In T. Parson and R. F. Bales *et al., The Family and Interaction Process.* New York: Free Press, 1955, pp. 259-306.

Baltzell, E. Digby. *Philadelphia Gentlemen.* Glencoe: The Free Press, 1958.

Bell, Daniel. *The Coming of Post-Industrial Society.* New York: Harper, 1973.

———. *The Cultural Contradictions of Capitalism.* New York: Basic Books, 1976

Bender, Marilyn. *The Beautiful People.* New York: Coward-McCann, 1967.

Benet, Mary. *The Secretarial Ghetto.* New York: McGraw-Hill, 1972.

Berger, Peter, Brigitte Berger, and H. Keliner. *The Homeless Mind.* New York: Vintage, 1973.

Bernard, Jessie. *The Future of Marriage.* New York: World, 1972.

———. *The Future of Motherhood.* New York: Dial, 1974.

———. "Talk, Conversation, Listening, Silence." In *The Sex Game.* New York: Atheneum, 1972, pp. 153-64.

Birmingham, Stephen. *The Right People.* Boston: Little, Brown, 1958.

Bledstein, Burton J. *The Culture of Professionalism.* New York: Norton, 1976.

Bowlby, John. *Maternal Care and Mental Health.* Geneva: World Health Organization, 1952.

Boyers, Robert (ed.). *Psychological Man.* New York: Harper, 1975.

Braverman, Harry. *Labor and Monopoly Capital.* New York: Monthly Review Press, 1974.

Brenton, Myron. *The American Male.* New York: Fawcett-Premier, 1966.

Britaan, Arthur. *The Privatized World.* London: Routledge, Kegan, Paul, 1977.

Brown, Bruce. *Marx, Freud and the Critique of Everyday Life.* New York: Monthly Review, 1973.

Burke, Thomas. *Dinner Is Served.* London: Butler and Tanner, 1937.

Centers, Richard. *The Psychology of Social Classes.* Princeton: Princeton University Press, 1949.

Chance, M. R. A., and Ray Larson (eds.). *The Social Structure of Attention.* New York: John Wiley, 1976.

Chessler, Phyllis. *Women and Madness.* New York: Doubleday, 1972.

Chodorow, Nancy. *The Social Reproduction of Mothering.* Berkeley University of California Press, 1977.

Coser, Rose Laug. "Laughter Among Colleagues." *Psychiatry,* 23(1960): 81-95.

de Beauvoir, Simone. *The Second Sex.* New York: Bantam, 1961. (First published, 1947.)

Durkheim, Émile. *The Division of Labor.* New York: Free Press, 1964.

———. *Suicide.* New York: Free Press, 1951.

Dworkin, Andrea. *Woman-Hating.* New York:

Ewen, Stewart. *Captains of Consciousness.* New York: McGraw-Hill, 1976.

Firestone, Shulamith. *The Dialectic of Sex.* New York: Bantam, 1970.

Frederick, Portia, and Carol Towner. *The Office Assistant.* Philadelphia: Saunders, 1956.

Freud, Sigmund. *On Narcissism.* London: Hogarth, 1957.

Friedan, Betty. *The Feminine Mystique.* New York: Dell, 1963.

Fromm, Erich. *Escape From Freedom.* New York: Avon, 1941.

———. *Man For Himself.* New York: Rinehart, 1947.

———. *The Sane Society.* New York: Rinehart and Winston, 1955.

Gerth, Hans, and C. Wright Mills. *Character and Social Structure.* New York: Oxford University Press, 1951.

Goffman, Erving. *Asylums.* New York: Anchor, 1961.

———. *Behavior in Public Places.* New York: Free Press, 1963.

———. *Interaction Ritual.* New York: Anchor, 1967.

———. *The Presentation of Self in Everyday Life.* New York: Anchor, 1959.

———. *Relations in Public.* New York: Harper, 1971.

Goldberg, Steven. *The Inevitability of Patriarchy.* New York: Morrow, 1973.

Gornick, Vivian, and B. K. Moran. *Woman in Sexist Society.* New York: Mentor, 1972.

Greer, Germaine. *The Female Eunuch.* New York: McGraw-Hill, 1971.

Habermas, Jurgen. *Legitimation Crisis.* Boston: Beacon Press, 1975.

Hare, A. Paul (ed.). *Handbook of Small Group Research.* Glencoe: Free Press, 1962.

Henry, Jules. *Pathways to Madness.* New York: Vintage, 1965.

Hilpert, Fred, Cheris Kramer, and Ruth Ann Clark, "Participants' Perception of Self and Partner in Mixed-Sex Dyads." *Central States, Speech Journal* (Spring 1975).

Hirschman, Lynette. "Analysis of Supportive and Assertive Behavior in Conversations." Paper presented at Linguistic Society of America, 1974.

_____ . "Female-Male Differences in Conversational Interaction." Paper presented at Linguistic Society of America, 1973.

Hoch, G. and R. Zubin (eds.). *Psychopathology of Communication.* New York: Grune and Stratton, 1958.

Howe, Louise Kapp. *Pink Collar Workers: Inside the World of Women's Work.* New York: Avon, 1977.

Jaccoby, Russell. *Social Amnesia.* Boston: Beacon Press, 1975.

Jackson, P.W. *Life in Classrooms.* New York: Holt, Rinehart and Winston, 1968.

Josephsons, Erich and Mary (eds.). *Man Alone.* New York: Dell, 1962.

Kahler, Erich. *The Tower and the Abyss.* New York: George Brazillier, 1957.

Karabel, Jerome. "Community Colleges and Social Stratification." *Harvard Educational Review* 42 (November 1972).

Kavaler, Lucy. *The Private Life of High Society.* New York: David McKay, 1960.

Keniston, Kenneth. *The Uncommitted.* New York: Harcourt, Brace & World, 1969.

Kenkel, William F. "Observational Studies of Husband-Wife Interaction Family Decision-Making." In M. Sussman (ed.) *Sourcebook in Marriage and the Family.* Boston: Houghton Mifflin, 1963, pp. 144-56.

Kernberg, Otto. "Factors in the Psychoanalytic Treatment of Narcissistic Personalities." *Journal of American Psychoanalytic Treatment,* 18, 1 (1970): 51-85.

Kohut, Heinz. *The Analysis of the Self.* New York: International University Press, 1971.

Kolko, Gabriel. *Wealth and Power in America.* New York: Praeger, 1962.

Komarovsky, Mirra. *Blue-Collar Marriage.* New York: Vintage, 1967.

Kraemer, Cheris. "Folklinguistics." *Psychology Today,* 8 (June 1974): 82-85.

_____ . "Sterotypes of Women's Speech: The Word from Cartoons." *Journal of Popular Culture* (1976).

Labov, William. *Sociolinguistic Patterns.* Philadelphia: University of Pennsylvania, 1972.

Laing, R. D. *The Divided Self.* London: Penguin, 1965.

Lasch, Christopher. *The Culture of Narcissism.* New York: Basic Books, 1978.

_____ . *Haven in a Troubled World.* New York: Basic Books, 1978.

_____ . "Narcissistic America." *New York Review of Books,* 22, 15 (September 1976): pp. 5-13.

Lefebvre, Henri. *Everyday Life in the Modern World.* London: Penguin, 1971.

Luckmann, Thomas and Peter Berger. "Social Mobility and Personal Identity." *European Journal of Sociology,* 5 (1964).

Lukacs, Georg. *History and Class-Consciousness.* Cambridge, Mass: MIT, 1971.

Lukes, Steven. *Individualism.* New York: Harper & Row, 1975.

Malcolm, Henry. *Generation of Narcissus.* Boston: Little, Brown, 1971.

Marcuse, Herbert. *One-Dimensional Man.* Boston: Beacon Press, 1964.

Marx, Karl. *Capital.* Volume 1. Translated by Samuel Moore and Edward Aveling. New York: Modern Library; first published 1906.

_____. and Friedrich Engels. *The German Ideology.* Moscow: Foreign Languages Publishing House, 1964.

Mills, C. Wright. *The Power Elite.* New York: Oxford, 1956.

_____. *The Sociological Imagination.* New York: Oxford, 1959.

_____. *White-Collar.* New York: Oxford, 1951.

Nisbet, Robert. *The Quest for Community.* New York: Oxford University Press, 1955.

Packard, Vance. *A Nation of Strangers.* New York: Pocket Books, 1974.

Parker, Angele. "Sex Differences in Classroom Intellectual Argumentation." M.S. thesis, Penn. State Univ., 1973.

Parker, Richard. *The Myth of the Middle Class.* New York: Harper & Row, 1972.

Pawley, Martin. *The Private Future.* New York: Pocket Books, 1977.

Piaget, Jean. *The Language and Thought of the Child.* New York: New American Library, 1974.

Pleck, Joseph and Jack Sawyer. *Men and Masculinity.* New York: Spectrum, 1974.

Post, Emily. *Etiquette.* New York: Funk and Wagnalls, 1973.

Poulantzas, Nicos. *Classes in Contemporary Capitalism.* London: New Left Books, 1975.

Reich, Wilhelm. *The Mass Psychology of Fascism.* New York: Noonday, 1970.

Reiff, Philip. *Fellow Teachers.* New York: Harper, 1973.

_____. *The Triumph of the Therapeutic.* New York: Harper & Row, 1966.

Reisman, David, Nathan Glazer, and Ruell Denny. *The Lonely Crowd.* New Haven: Yale University Press, 1950.

Rohman, Mary. "Conversations: Male and Female Experience." Mimeographed, Boston, 1975.

Rosenthal, Robert, and Lenore Jacobson. *Pygmalion in the Classroom.* New York: Holt, Rinehart and Winston, 1968.

Rowbatham, Sheila. *Woman's Consciousness; Man's World.* London: Pelican, 1974.

Schaar, John. *Escape From Authority: The Perspectives of Erich Fromm.* New York: Harper, 1964.

Schrank, Robert. *Ten-Thousand Working Days.* Cambridge, Mass.: MIT Press, 1978.

Schroyer, Trent. *The Critique of Domination.* New York: George Brazillier, 1973.

Sennett, Richard. *The Fall of Public Man.* New York: Knopf, 1977.

_____. *The Uses of Disorder.* New York: Vintage. 1970.

_____ (ed.). *Classic Essays on the Culture of Cities.* New York: Meredith, 1969.

_____, and Jonahtan Cobb. *The Hidden Injuries of Class.* New York: Knopf, 1973.

[Seventeen Magazine]. *The New Seventeen Book of Young Living.* New York: Houpt, 1970.

Shuy, Roger, Walter A. Wolfram, and William K. Riley, *Linguistic Correlates of Social Stratification in Detroit Speech.* Final Report, Project 6-1347. Washington, D.D.: U. S. Office of Education, 1967.

Simmel, Georg. *The Sociology of Georg Simmel,* K. Wolff (ed.). New York: Free Press, 1950.

Slater, Philip. "Culture, Sexuality and Narcissism." In his *Footholds: Understanding the Shifting Family and Sexual Tensions in Our Culture.* New York: Dutton, 1977.

_____. *Earthwalk.* New York: Doubleday, 1974.

_____. *The Pursuit of Loneliness.* Boston: Beacon Press, 1970.

Soskin, William and Vera P. John. "The Study of Spontaneous Talk." In Roger Barker (ed.), *The Stream of Behavior.* New York: Appleton-Century-Crofts, 1963.

Spitz, René. "Anaclitic Depression." *Psychoanalytic Study of the Child* 2 (1946): 313-342.

Strodtbeck, Fred. "Husband-Wife Interaction over Revealed Differences." *American Sociological Review,* 16 (1951): 468-73.

_____, and Richard Mann. "Sex-Role Differentiation in Jury Deliberations." *Sociometry,* 19 (1956): 3 11.

_____, et al. "Social Status in Jury Deliberations." *American Sociological Review,* 22(1957): 713-19.

Tepperman, Jean. *Not Servants, Not Machines: Office-Workers Speak Out.* Boston: Beacon Press, 1976.

Terkel, Studs. *Working.* New York: Avon, 1972.

Thorne, Barrie. "Women in the Draft Resistance Movement: A Case Study of

Sex-Roles and Social Movements." *Sex-Roles: A Journal of Research,* 1, 2 (1975).

_____, and Nancy Henley (eds.). *Language and Sex.* Rowley, Mass: Newbury House Publishers, 1975.

Toennies, Frederick. *Community and Society.* East Lansing, Michigan: Michigan State University Press, 1957.

Trudgill, Peter. "Sex, Covert Prestige and Linguistic Change in the Urban British English of Norwich." In *Language and Society.* Cambridge: Cambridge University Press, 1972, pp. 179-95.

Turnbull, Colin. *The Mountain People.* New York: Touchstone, 1972.

Vaughan, W. and E. McGinnies. "Some Biographical Determiners of Participation in Group Discussion." *Journal of Applied Psychology* 41 (1957): 179-85.

Veblen, Thorstein. *The Portable Veblen,* edited by Max Lerner. New York: Viking, 1948.

_____. *The Theory of the Leisure Class.* New York: 1889.

Weber, Max. *Economy and Society,* edited by G. Roth and C. Wittich. New York: Bedminster Press, 1968.

Whyte, William. *Men at Work.* Homewood, Illinois: Dorsey Press, 1961.

Wilde, Oscar. *The Fairy Tales of Oscar Wilde.* New York: Hart, 1975.

Wirth, Louis. *On Cities and Social Life,* edited by A. J. Reiss, Chicago: University of Chicago Press, 1964.

Zaretsky, Eli. *Capitalism, The Family and Personal Life.* New York: Harper, 1974.

Zimmerman, Don H. and Candace West. "Sex-Roles, Interruptions and Silences in Conversation." In Barrie Thorne and Nancy Henley (eds.), *Language and Sex.* Rowley, Mass.: Newbury House Press, 1975, pp. 105-129.

Index